Skywriting

RANDOM HOUSE
NEW YORK

Skywriting

A LIFE OUT OF THE BLUE

Jane Pauley

Printed in the United States of America on acid-free paper
Random House website address: www.atrandom.com

246897531

FIRST EDITION

Book design by Carole Lowenstein

To

Ann,	*Garry,*
who was always	*who always will be*
there	

and

Rickie, Ross, and Tom,

my inspiration

To

Ann,   *Garry,*
who was always   *who always will be*
there

and
Rickie, Ross, and Tom,
my inspiration

Contents

PREFACE

Truth arrives in microscopic increments, and when enough has accumulated, in a moment of recognition, you just know. You know because the truth fits.

I was the only member of my family to lack the gene for numbers, but I do need things to add up. Approaching midlife, I became aware of a darkening feeling—was it something heavy on my heart or was something missing? Grateful as I am for the opportunities I've had, and especially for the people who came into my life as a result, I couldn't ignore that feeling. I had the impulse to begin a conversation with myself, through writing, as if to see whether my fingers could get to the bottom of it.

It was a Saturday morning eight or ten years ago when I began following this impulse to find the answers to unformed questions. Skywriting is what I call my personal process of discovery, because it seemed that I plied blue sky—so much of the work went on unconsciously. I imagined the "boys in the back room" toiling while I slept, because often I knew things in the morning that I hadn't known the night before. Writers sometimes say they write to see what their fingers know; my fingers seemed to have their own agenda.

It was a fascinating exercise, but in time I started to wonder what the point was—was I headed somewhere or just doomed to wander? Frustrated, I described my writing process as "wandering purposelessly."

When I encountered that phrase years later in an inverted form—"purposeful wandering"—I recognized its significance immediately. It turned "wandering purposelessly" on its head.

"Purposeful wandering" is to be actively available to moments of recognition—the portals to insight. Words in frequent rotation in our heads, such as *purposeless,* aren't circling in and out of our consciousness for no reason, nor are fragments of songs, or the snapshot images from long ago, burned into an otherwise faulty memory. They are expressions of unconscious meaning, and I think of them as moments of pre-recognition.

For instance, why did the discovery of a red swizzle stick in my father's suitcase give me a bad feeling as a little girl, and why was the memory engraved on my brain? It had significance just beyond the reach of my understanding. Nothing stronger than ginger ale was ever served in our house; I liked mine in a martini glass. Nobody but me ever reached for that set of martini glasses in the top cupboard. A swizzle stick with a martini-glass decoration on the top didn't belong in Daddy's suitcase; it didn't fit us. This was a moment of pre-recognition. Many years later, recognition arrived amidst a bundle of evidence my sister, Ann, and I could not ignore—it fit the truth.

When I was still little, a doctor told my mother that "Jane is a nervous child, and she'll have to be careful her whole life." I was sitting on the examination table, listening. I didn't ask *why* or *how*—much less, would a career in television be okay? I don't know what symptoms provoked the visit or what the doctor meant by "nervous," but I'm pretty sure there was a correlation between those childhood "nerves" and an EKG tape forty years later that inspired my doctor to say, "I don't see this much tension in twenty women!" She didn't get it. I didn't, either. I was happily married, with three lovely kids, dogs, a successful career—a perfect picture. What was wrong with it?

The mental landscape of my life when I set out on this Sky-writing mission most resembled an early map of the New World, with great expanses of terra incognita. There were childhood memories as vivid as a clump of tar stuck to my Red Ball Jets in the summer after the road was paved. My bedroom was intact, down to what I called the "polio shirts" in the "chester drawers." The Beatles' arrival in 1964 was crystal-clear, but the previous year, when my mother had cancer, was missing. There was a pattern in my family of missing years and missing persons. I needed to get to the bottom of it.

There were no pictures of my paternal grandparents in our house. I didn't know what my father's mother looked like, though I was named for her: Margaret Pauley. How could I be such a strenuously committed "realist" (I even prefer to read nonfiction) despite such a tentative grasp on reality? A moment of recognition arrives when a conviction (I'm a realist) meets a contradiction (I didn't even know what my grandmother looked like). A little girl might develop an attachment to what's real *because* of all she doesn't know, not despite it. Skywriting has become an accumulation of moments of clarity in which I finally saw what had been in plain sight all along.

"Just look on the bright side" strikes me as an essentially pessimistic point of view. I can't deny the research that says optimists live longer, but I think they lack the faith to take life whole, and it comes no other way. I like to think that *Skywriting* is about looking *toward* the bright side, knowing the journey there will not be a straight line but rather a spiraling path that moves forward in a pattern of turning back—purposeful wandering. Here's where the realist in me is revealed for an optimist, because I believed in my future enough to risk finding that my idea of my past had been something of a fantasy. As long as it was my only story, I had no choice but to stick to it. I was changed the moment I recognized that the absence of a story doesn't mean there is no story.

• • •

Three years ago, I suffered the first significant illness of my life; I was diagnosed with bipolar disorder. It was medically induced by treatment for something that sounds utterly innocuous—hives.

The cause of the hives was, and is still, a mystery; I suspect it wasn't one factor but a whole gang of them. Menopause looms large at my age, but so does being a mother with children growing up, being a daughter without parents. I hear a biological clock ticking again—how should I spend the rest of my life? I'd like not to spend it with more tension than twenty women. I read recently that "many people don't know which elements of their lives cause stress and which they actually enjoy." My illness compelled me to pay attention to what my body was trying to tell me.

Have you noticed that the happy endings in fairy tales were predicated on unhappy beginnings? In no version of the story does Cinderella have a happy childhood, or a life of "placid conventionality" as I had, in the well-chosen words of a young writer named Frank Rich. In 1977, when I was twenty-six, he interviewed me in my office at the *Today* show and my parents at home in Indianapolis. He found my office "devoid of personality," and our home did nothing to alter the impression. He was not being unkind. He spoke for both of us when he wrote, "I don't get it." He could not figure out how someone so unaggressive, more like Dinah Shore than Lesley Stahl, as he put it, could get to the top of a competitive profession so young and so fast. I agreed; it seemed like I had won it in a contest. I knew I had not reached the pinnacle by pluck, and I didn't really believe in luck. I am such a hard-core realist that even my daydreams have to be plausible! It was my life that stretched credulity.

For thirty-two years, a career on television has been as inseparable from me as my shadow. It has been an uneasy coexistence. I'd almost given up trying to explain my mixed feelings for a career that by any objective consideration was fabulous. My psyche didn't relate to "objective consideration" and persisted in sending messages—including depression and probably hives—that corrective measures should be taken. I get it now. *Skywriting* will challenge the spun-sugar underpinnings of my career.

My first night in a hospital bed, I cried for my father. He must have felt this way, too. He must have mourned the person he thought he was, just like I mourned "Janie," the person I had thought I was—the "most normal girl on TV"—the girl who never was. When I got well, I realized there was some truth to that: Jane had to be discovered. *Skywriting* is about that discovery.

PART I

Out
of the Blue

May 2001

The room was nice. Large and sunny. Inviting, almost. The layout was defined by three rectangles. One was an entry large enough to be a vestibule, which lent the space an aura of privacy. It opened into the principal area, but there was a little niche off to the side—so instead of a room with four walls, there were eight, and instead of four corners, there were six, plus the private bath. It gave the room a cozy complexity.

But the showstoppers were the two large windows facing east and two more facing south, which framed the Fifty-ninth Street Bridge a quarter of a mile or so away—the one immortalized by Simon and Garfunkel. It spanned the East River ten floors below.

New York City would never have a lazy river, would it? This one flows energetically to the south and then turns right around and flows to the north.... All day long it goes back and forth, back and forth, with the big Atlantic Ocean tides. Fast, but still not too fast for the ferries, which roar back and forth, insensible to the havoc left in their jumbo wake. Only the little tugboats go slowly— nudging enormous tankers through a narrow strip of commerce that never gets snarled like the three lanes of traffic heading south on the FDR Drive. It's just the opposite of the song: The lanes heading north are on a lower level, so in effect the Bronx is down and the Battery's up. I'm smack in midtown, the busiest place on earth—rush hour is every hour of the day, and sometimes the night.

And, of course, the sun moves around a lot, too, rising over Randalls Island with my breakfast, then climbing higher and higher. For lunch, it turns toward the Chrysler Building, and then down and out of sight. Every day. But I'm not going anywhere.

This was my home for three weeks in the spring of 2001.

My tides were fluctuating, too—back and forth, back and forth—sometimes so fast they seemed to be spinning. They call this "rapid cycling." It's a marvel that a person can appear to be standing still when the mood tides are sloshing back and forth, sometimes sweeping in both directions at once. They call that a "mixed state." It felt like a miniature motocross race going on in my head. It made a little hum, and my eyes sort of burned and felt a little too large for their sockets.

But it was a lovely room. When I checked in, late in May, I was lucky to get it. Evidently there were no other VIPs in residence at that time—not at this address, at least. I was allowed to bypass the usual chaos at admitting, a nod to my potential to be recognized, and though technically I was a patient at Payne Whitney Psychiatric Clinic, I was installed in a room on a general floor, another nod to my singularity. I never saw it, but I heard that the other floor had locked doors, that psychiatric patients were supposed to wear hospital gowns rather than the fancy pajamas I was given liberty to wear.

The special attention and fine accommodations had not been at my request, nor was I here because I wanted to show off my nice pj's. I was here because they said I ought to be—I accepted that much—and had come, under my own steam, for a few days.

I became accustomed to mealtime trays with plastic utensils and no knives, to leaving the bathroom door open at least a crack, to sleeping with a lady in white sitting six feet away in the darkness, keeping an eye on me. No hands under the covers, she said on my first night away from home, which made me cry—acutely aware of where I was and why. I cried a little harder.

In time, my lovely, sunny room, with African violets thriving under my personal care in the morning light, came to feel like home. And I had to wear pajamas only at night—sweats and T-shirts seemed perfectly appropriate for casual entertaining in my room with a view.

March 1999

Hives: I used to call them the seven-year itch, because they had first appeared when I was seven, then again at fourteen and, briefly, again when I was twenty-one. That last time, just before I finished college, everyone had a case of nerves: My roommates were either hyperventilating, suffering migraines, or getting married. When I was twenty-eight—at the next seven-year interval—the hives were silent and, I thought, gone for good.

Out of the blue, in March 1999, while I was on vacation with my family and six months shy of my forty-ninth birthday, my unwelcome friends came back for the first time in my adult life and settled. I didn't see them every day, but often enough that any day they could show up for no reason. These were not red, patchy, itchy everyday hives; mine involved soft-tissue swelling in odd places such as the pads of my fingers and feet or the pressure point from a bracelet, but most typically on an upper eyelid or my lips—places most incompatible with a career on camera.

That would be the least of it.

Chronic recurrent idiopathic urticaria edema is the full name—a diagnosis more worthy of all the attention. After I first spoke publicly about it, scores of people wrote to me, thinking—mistakenly—that, being a TV personality, Jane Pauley would have been given the cure. I had not. But for me, as it turned out, the treatment was far worse than the disease.

April 2000

"We have to smack them down!" my doctor had said after my first trip to the ER. Steroids were the weapons of choice—the anti-inflammatory kind, not the bodybuilding kind, but it felt like a heavy dose of testosterone nonetheless. It was not a decision made lightly; these are powerful drugs that have to be taken in slowly increasing increments over a period of weeks. Tapering off is done in similar increments. The steroids had the desired effect—the hives subsided—but as a side effect of the drugs, I was revved!

I was so energized that I didn't just walk down the hall, I felt like I was motoring down the hall. I was suddenly the equal of my high-energy friends who move fast and talk fast and loud. I told everyone that I could understand why men felt like they could run the world, because I felt like that. This was a new me, and I liked her!

Earlier that spring, I had had a modest idea for a voter registration drive at New York City's High School for Leadership and Public Service, where I was "principal for a day." The faculty, staff, and kids ran with the idea—fifty-two students were added to the voter rolls at lunchtime in the cafeteria. It was very moving.

Later, I was back at the same high school, with a bigger idea. After weeks of steroids, I had a more ambitious agenda—a ramped-up voter registration drive. It would be like the first one, but instead of confining the drive to the cafeteria, I said, "Let's do it citywide!" Two thousand New York City school kids were registered before school was out.

May–June 2000

It was nearly midnight, and I could see the flashing lights approaching our apartment building from two blocks away—a fire truck and an ambulance. I was both relieved and embarrassed. My throat was swelling up. My doctor had suggested I call 911 instead of looking for a taxi to the hospital. I had called 911, but I didn't anticipate a convoy.

Before long, the doorbell rang and I went to answer it, finding two paramedics—a Hispanic woman and a black man, both middle-aged and experienced-looking—standing at the door with two very big bags, ready to save a life.

"Where's the patient?" they asked.

"It's me," I said sheepishly. Any kind of swelling that involves air passageways, I've learned, is taken pretty seriously by doctors. It has the potential to be life-threatening. But at that moment, with the flashing lights and the vehicles double-parked outside, somehow "potential" didn't justify the response.

One paramedic went straight to the paperwork. The other tied off my upper arm and took a vial of blood. She apologized as she inserted a plastic tube in a vein. At first it burned, and a stinging sensation raced all the way up my arm and flooded my throat with a sudden heat. Warmth filled my belly, and I felt safe in the competent hands of this experienced team. But on the ride in the ambulance I was aware that most people strapped in that gurney aren't feeling as comfy-cozy as I was. When we arrived at the hospital, I saw three uniformed paramedics rush to the door, and all I could think was how preposterous it was: "Make way! Make way! HIVES!"

• • •

The steroids worked, until I stopped taking them. So I started a second round, and by June they were smacking me down! Instead of feeling powerful, I was just irritable. Instead of motoring me down the hall, my engine was just revving. I was going nowhere. It was hard to work, and I was exhausted. *Dateline* executive producer Neal Shapiro gave me two weeks to chill out and relax. I told a colleague that when I came back I wouldn't be talking so loud. I barely worked during the summer of 2000.

The hives came and went, but that was incidental to the depression I could feel gathering around me. At the end of the summer, I was sent to a psychopharmacologist. He prescribed a low-dose antidepressant and promised that I'd feel better "in weeks." When I didn't, he said, "Well, certainly by Thanksgiving." After that, he stopped making promises. I sank lower and lower. I knew the difference between an afternoon nap and three hours in bed, two hours of which weren't even spent sleeping, but just sinking into a state of captivity.

January 2001

The doctor was frustrated and surprised that I hadn't responded to the antidepressant. I was only getting worse, even with a different dosage. He recommended that I transition slowly to a promising new medication. The buzz on Wall Street was sending the company's stock through the roof. But after years of being the patient who defied every doctor's predictions, I didn't get my hopes up.

• • •

On the fifty-second floor at NBC, there are executive suites and large conference rooms with sweeping views of New York that offer startling confirmation that Manhattan really is an island, a magnificent partnership between sky and skyline. And you feel on top of it. It's a heady sensation—but by January 2001, I was feeling something new.

It was a party for people who had twenty-five years with the company—and, incredibly, I was one of them. I arrived with my usual resistance, shyness, inertia—but as I almost always do, I was soon thinking, *I'm having a nice time!* Making small talk didn't seem such an effort. And chatting with Andy Lack, then president of NBC News, I felt unusually "on." Finally, falling into an animated conversation with a *New York Times* reporter, I talked about my plans for writing a book, and she promised to send me a copy of her new novel, *Glory*. But I had a disquieting feeling that I had been a little carried away with myself.

I'm very conservative about medicine—I don't even take aspirin casually. So when the doctor said to take it slow—gradually reduce the dose of the first medication while adding small increments of the new one—I went extra slow. After three weeks, I hadn't exceeded 5 mg of the new prescription, but I could feel a big change. I had energy, for one thing, and ideas—many ideas. A show. A book. A magazine.

February 2001

My husband, Garry, was becoming concerned. When I started talking about my own line of clothing, his concern upgraded to alarm. The better I felt, it seemed to me, the worse he felt about it. I accused him of being happier when I was depressed. Everyone else seemed delighted. My agent, Wayne Kabak, had never seen me more energized and engaged. While full-throttle drive and ambition weren't the norm for me, they were for everyone else on his client list. I'd always been the exception. My calendar for February was filling up with meetings. But March, April, and May were completely, deliciously blank.

Three years before, during my last contract negotiation, I had asked for time instead of money. If anyone at NBC had ever done such a thing, I wasn't aware of it, but I had the idea that we could take the children to Europe for the whole summer; I had heard there were families who did things like that. Alas, mine wasn't one of them. The kids were horrified: "She's not going to make us do that, is she, Dad?" I surrendered. But I still had the time coming to me. I remembered it now, and it seemed just what I needed.

Asking only that I wait until the end of the key ratings period in February, Neal Shapiro generously agreed. He didn't argue, as he could have, that the time period agreed to in the contract had been summer, not the regular TV season. Neal may have noticed something; Andy Lack did. After the party, he went to Tom Brokaw: "You know Jane so well. Is she okay?" I was starting to wonder myself. It seemed harder and harder to prepare for an interview—I either procrastinated or I wasn't able to concentrate. I was of two minds about my new persona. On the one hand I was impressed with my new creative energy, but on the other hand I was suspicious that I didn't have it completely under control. Sometimes I was raring to go; other times, just hanging on. I desperately wanted that sabbatical.

I was entitled to ten weeks but got a bonus. *Dateline* was pre-empted the entire week preceding the official start of my sabbatical. I didn't waste a moment of it, arranging to accompany my sister on a business trip to Boca Raton. While she worked, I relaxed or wrote or read a little. I finished *Glory*—and liked it a lot. I was also in the market for real estate and roamed around the

Internet looking for something nearby for my mother-in-law. I found a cottage she would have adored, but the timing was wrong for her. So I bought it for myself!

Garry could relax, knowing that Ann was keeping an eye on me. She assured him that I was great. He wasn't very reassured. He said the doctor had asked him how I was sleeping. Funny he would ask, I thought. I had so much energy—even after dinner. I wasn't at all sleepy, and the night before, I'd been up till midnight. That night at one A.M., after Ann had gone to sleep, I was not only awake but completely alert. Frankly, I did think that was a little odd.

I'd been reading books about management and organizations for a long time, recreationally. On our February trip to Boca Raton, my sister recommended *Now, Discover Your Strengths*, by Marcus Buckingham and Donald O. Clifton, who argue that it's far more productive to develop a strength than to strengthen a weakness. A provocative idea—assuming I had strengths. I was dubious.

I went online and, with the pass-code that came with the book, registered and answered the questions. Experts call it a "testing instrument"—it's not apparent to a layperson like me how the questions produce accurate results. Instantly, I got mine and my first thought was that I didn't recognize this person they said I was.

My strengths were as strong as a cup of espresso. This was definitely *not* my self-image: Janie, the delightful little girl. I alone didn't see the resemblance; Garry, Ann, the kids, friends—everyone else smiled with recognition, and they even had evidence to back it up. How was it possible to present one way and feel the opposite?

The first sign of trouble brewing was that my strengths were finally growing palpable even to me. Back in New York, on the first Monday of my sabbatical, I buzzed into my doctor's office,

settled into the chair, and rattled off the events of my busy weekend, along with all my plans! I was darn proud that I'd not
wasted a minute. At the end of the session, he said, "You're a little hyper." And he called Garry and said, "Your wife is very sick."

He scheduled an urgent visit with the psychopharmacologist, who
asked me if I'd made any big decisions or major purchases. Dropping my head and my voice, I said, "Well, I bought a house." He
knew immediately what had happened. He explained that he had
prescribed an antidepressant for a common unipolar depression I
was evidently suffering from. It had unmasked a never-before-
suspected vulnerability to bipolar depression. Strongly heritable,
the disease was unknown in my family, though it might have ex-
isted below the radar. (The idea of mania in my family is almost
laughable.) But in a person with bipolar disease, an antidepressant, without the addition of a mood-stabilizing medication, can
be dangerous. It produces a bungee-cord effect. From the depths
of depression, a person can be flung to the heights of mania and,
inevitably, to the depths again, and so on, in a wild wave of ups
and downs. That it took five months to provoke the mood swings
also known as manic depression was pretty surprising. And four
months on steroids before that!

Steroids—they're another thing you would be cautious in giving to a person at risk of bipolar disease. The months on steroids
had produced a milder sequence of highs and lows. In fact, the
steroids are what drove me to tears. And what drove me to steroids
was hives.

The doctor was frankly not enthusiastic about seeing his patient haplessly turn herself into the poster child for manic-
depressive disease and advised me to tell my boss that I would
extend my eight-week sabbatical into a medical leave of absence
due to a thyroid disorder that needed attention. This had the ad-

vantage of being true, if not the entire truth. Instead of taking his advice, I informed him I was already writing a book!

The rush of ideas that had impressed many people and worried Garry was symptomatic of *hypomania.* This was a new word for me, which I interpreted—incorrectly—to mean "big-time mania." I knew that manic-depressive disorder was now called bipolar disorder. The little I knew about it came from Sally Field's portrayal of a psychotic mother in full-blown mania on the TV show *ER.* I never visited that place, thank God. When I looked up *hypomania* (*hypo* meaning "mild," not big-time), I recognized myself right away.

On new medication, I was told to expect to be back out of the deep woods in a couple of weeks. What a godsend to be able to recuperate in privacy. Working on "the book" at least gave each day some structure and purpose. I could write all morning long, literally. One day I wondered: Why had I thought *Skyrocketing* was such a good idea for a title? Books and newspapers, even my own writing, were hard to read, a symptom of hypomania, but material came spewing forth unedited.

Feelings came shooting in and out at the speed of bullet trains, along with ideas, followed by phone calls that produced action plans. My mind was racing. Mostly it was good, but I was aware that I was in hyper mode from the moment I woke up at six-thirty and started the day with a bang. When the phone rang at about eight o'clock one morning, it felt like half the day was already done, and I asked my mother-in-law if I could change phones because I was standing in the utility room with a hammer in my hand. Me wandering the house with a hammer in my hand had become almost a metaphor for my home life.

This was not the sabbatical I had planned, filled with meetings reading, and travel. I told Wayne Kabak not to schedule anything, explaining that doctors said I had too many ideas circling, and too close together. He understood, but assured me they were good ideas nonetheless. My afternoons were free and I still had energy to burn and money to spend. I was seen around town, generally alone, and often in department stores.

One day, when I was prowling a room filled with marked-down home furnishings, a young clerk asked me if I liked red and showed me three different red pillows. On sale. I picked up the smallest one and, feeling rather proud of how knowing and womanly I sounded, said, "A little red goes a long way."

I went back to the gym for the first time in months—to get my nails done. I've never been much of a manicure lady, not since I was told in an interview on *Today* twenty years ago how much time and money I'd be saving if I skipped weekly manicures.

On my way to my locker, NBC correspondent Betty Rollin happened by, wearing nothing but a towel and looking darn cute in it. I probably violated some code of the locker room when I said, "Hi, Betty. I've never seen you seminude before!" By then, I was wearing ten sparkling fingernails and ten sparkling toenails and shuffling noisily in a pair of paper-bag shoes. Otherwise, I was still fully clothed and in the company of a locker-room attendant, who had insightfully taken on the tone of a hospital orderly as she guided me to my locker. I did remember where it was, but after so many months, I had no hope of remembering my locker combination. When I got it open and saw my makeup bag, the shower bag, and the mesh bag with my clean shorts and shirt and socks just back from the laundry (four seasons ago), and my shoes and other odd stuff, I felt like I'd come by to clean out the earthly goods of some departed soul. What a forlorn assortment of stuff I'd left behind. I felt so sad.

As I stood before my locker, realizing that I'd had a vulnerability to bipolar disorder, that I was suffering now from hypomania, I recognized the symptoms from long before I ever knew I was having symptoms. In fact, wasn't it only a month ago, sitting at my sister's kitchen table, that I had asked a provocative question: What is it about us Pauley sisters, a couple of Midwestern girls? We seem to like it up here on the high wire.

I don't think a stranger would have noticed anything remarkable—I wasn't swinging from the chandelier. It was a spectrum of agitation that could pass before your eyes in a single conversation. But the turbulence affected the whole family. Although the villain was the illness and the victim was me, only a doctor could make such a distinction. My daughter, Rickie, was the most overtly affected by an alien presence. She did battle with it openly, which is to say, with me. She seemed to think I was trying to get away with something. She deduced that Garry was the default target of my anger and aligned herself with him like a little Athena.

I was sensitive about giving the appearance of grandiosity, like a person who knows he's straddling the line between being sober and being a little drunk and wonders whether it's obvious when he orders the next drink. But the new cottage gave me a cover for shopping—sheets and pillows and wool blankets (on sale in April!), coffee mugs (on sale!), orchids (on sale!)—and prowling for bargains surely made all the shopping seem only 40 percent "off."

In a memo to the architect, I described a dozen ideas; none are outrageous, and some are pretty good. But I can now see that together they add up to more than the sum of their parts. I appear to be self-conscious about that, and with subtle phrasing try to minimize the impact: Instead of ideas, for instance, I call them "goals." I acknowledge "having already gotten ahead of myself" and doing something "but within reason." I emphasize the modesty of my ambition with references to "cottage-scale," "cottage-like," and "charming-no-drama." And finally (fobbing this idea off on a little girl), I mention that my daughter wants me to ask: Is there nowhere on this hilly terrain for a pool?

I learned that the manic side of the manic–depressive combo is, weirdly, linked to a shopping impulse. As Garry put it, the druggist who sells lithium knows he's likely to sell a few other items, too. I did have a robust hunting–and–gathering impulse. Garry had marveled at the service I provided local merchants that spring, mopping up their excess merchandise before tax time. That was later, when he finally understood what was happening. Before, it had been only one more symptom that his wife was becoming a person he couldn't recognize. "It seems like you're trying to buy happiness," he'd said.

I knew I wasn't well, but I didn't seem to be at serious risk for more than some turbulence, though my doctors alluded to the possibility of a hard landing. I never had morbid thoughts. I never suffered the severe kind of depressive disorder that William Styron and others have written so movingly about.

From an e–mail:

Speaking of the blues. The most important thing I can do now for my family is face the fact that my depression is the first major illness of our marriage. Having seen my parents go into long, alternating treatment and recovery modes, I know the drill.

Back in January, I had interviewed a teenage girl, along with her parents; they'd had no idea that their daughter—a star student, athlete, leader—had been fantasizing about ways to kill herself. She had settled on a leap from the Chesapeake Bay Bridge—the equivalent of a ten-story building. But because her instincts as a competitive swimmer carried her into the water with minimum impact, she survived. Until she read a magazine article in the hospital listing symptoms she was intimately familiar with, she never knew she was depressed. That's why she and her family appeared on *Dateline*—to get the word out about what depression looks like, that a depressed girl can look pretty normal, and that having suicidal thoughts is dangerous. The thing I simply could not comprehend was how the girl thought her family could live without her.

Heading home in the back of a cab one day, absentmindedly looking at small white clouds moving across the blue sky, I suddenly understood. I imagined a hole opening up in the sky; slipping through it, a person could simply be forgotten.

Later that day, I explained this to my doctor. He responded by asking if I thought I'd feel better in the hospital. I wasn't thinking about killing myself, but for my doctor, just thinking about suicide was coming too close to the precipice. The next morning, I checked into Payne Whitney.

My door was always open. Pychiatrists making rounds arrived all day long—singly, in pairs or clusters, even in groups. Most of them were either young or incredibly young; the younger they were, the longer they stayed. Everyone's favorite topic was me.

They asked simple, dispassionate questions like "How are you?" which I answered in voluminous and passionate detail. What a star patient—so verbal and insightful. I was uniquely equipped to help them work out our problem.

In that hospital, *How are you?* is not small talk. It's the operative question—because how I was changed from hour to hour. Inquiring about my state of mind was the equivalent of taking my temperature in determining how I was doing.

My discursive style, my facility with metaphor—along with the five pages of notes I'd taken since their last visit—would certainly help us get to the source of our trouble very quickly. These visits were the most interesting part of my day, and I flattered myself that I was the most interesting part of theirs—not thinking through the implications of being the "most interesting" in a psychiatric hospital. But it was something of a surprise, when the first Friday came, to realize how much the doctors were looking forward to the weekends! They needed a break from me and the fifty-nine patients upstairs.

I learned that weekends are basically about keeping the patients from degrading too far before the first string returns on Monday morning. One Sunday morning, two young residents arrived for a chat. Typically, most of them had never heard of *Dateline*, so we usually had some catching up to do. Being the youngest staffers, they had the time to do it. (I learned to read the body language of the others; when it was time for them to go, I'd speed up the information. *Velocity:* a bucket with a wider pour-spout.) When they looked at their watches, it meant I had to talk fast. All they saw was a woman talking fast.

I looked pretty good, frankly. I had nothing but time in the mornings, and company was coming, so I went to a little trouble. One good hair day after another. My daytime look was either a black or white boatneck cotton pullover with three-quarter-length sleeves—I had several clean ones in my drawer at all times, and that made me feel better. I wore gray draw-string pants in a soft, never-wrinkle fabric. I'd fold my tailored cotton pajamas carefully so they'd be crisp, and put them away in their own drawer—the pink ones were more flattering, but the green ones were softer. Both pairs had been very expensive before the markdowns. I was glad to have them—I shudder to think about my usual nightwear. Around the house I'm gener-ally barefoot; hospital floors are clean but cold, so I usually wore a pair of straw slippers there. I even wore a tiny bit of makeup—but nothing that would smear if I spent any time in bed, face buried in a pillow.

Because I felt so vulnerable, looking normal helped bridge the gap between the person I was searching for and this healthy-looking woman in the mirror, who had a special nurse stationed in a chair near her bed around the clock—and who had to keep the bathroom door open, at least a crack. I was in the hospital under an assumed name—Margaret Grandison—as if people who recognize me couldn't put the right name to my face anyway! People were in and out all day with the rolling blood pressure stand and vials for blood and thermometers and meds and mops and buckets and trays. But after a week or ten days, people started calling me Jane. And there was some curiosity—I didn't seem sick, my meds weren't familiar, and I had a fake name. The question *What are you in for?* came one way or another. Even though they knew my real name, I was a mystery patient.

If you didn't know me well, you might not have noticed anything strange; I was strange only for me. New Yorkers, by reputation, are fast-talking, assertive, and easily annoyed; I fit right in. All of my normal emotional states, from sad to angry, were intensified—but never pathologically so. I was never manic as I'd always understood the word. Sally Field's brilliant portrayal on *ER* was being rerun while I was in the hospital. I couldn't watch.

I had already decided that if only one good thing came out of this mess it would be the opportunity to talk about the disease. It didn't seem like an act of courage. No one I cared about was likely to love me less—virtually all of our friends and the whole family already knew. Beyond that, it seemed as easy as writing a big check to the United Way; I could afford it. Most people living courageously with mental illness fear losing everything—they can't afford to give people the benefit of the doubt. I can. It seemed pretty simple.

"Hospitals are crazy-making places," according to the doctor who ran the place, and he was anxious to send me home. While my discharge and reentry were being discussed, I just looked down at the floor, at three pairs of men's shoes: all black. I was being sent home, ready or not, and I didn't think I was ready. I was starting to feel right at home there—being taken care of isn't that hard to get used to. Even having a nurse sit up all night by your bed stops being so weird after you get to know her a little bit. (Unless she snores.) She also had a daytime counterpart—and if I moved from the bed to the little sofa in the niche, then the nurse would move a little closer, too. But in time the rules relaxed—and then my companions went away altogether. I was getting better!

I lived alone—meals and meds delivered; long, relaxed conversations about my favorite subject: me. I had e-mail. TV. Telephone. CDs. My watercolors. And the sun in the morning and the moon at night. I sometimes sat at the window and enjoyed the view. It never dawned on me that guests in psychiatric wards arouse suspicion by doing that—even if the windows are locked.

Summer 2001

One dreamy day in the summer of 2001, at the shore, I was mesmerized by a trio of opposing ripples weaving undulating crosswise patterns at the water's edge, when a word floated up with an exclamation point: *crosscurrents!* Nature is full of these unsettled places where the seams show—playful as dancing dust devils, menacing as a clap of thunder, compelling as a perfect storm. From my hospital window, I had studied eddies—river dimples carried by the current but paying it no mind—and as I did so, I was a swirling body of indecision. I didn't recognize the metaphor, but I see it now: a mood up meeting a mood down; they collide and spin, locked in a duel until they break apart. Rapid cycling.

I hadn't been bipolar all along. I had had no symptoms that would have alerted the half dozen doctors involved in prescribing medications to me. I was just a lady with hives. But steroids and antidepressants can be like nitroglycerine to a person with a vulnerability to bipolar. And on top of it all, I still had hives! Hives that had defied doctors of every medical specialty for two years. Why?

Eventually, I thought to wonder what I had been doing at work in 1999 when the hives had suddenly reappeared after thirty–five years. I searched the files on my computer back to March 1999, and there was the answer: Daddy.

Bipolarity would not have happened to me had it not been for the hives. The fact that it came with a stigma attached to it made me feel for Daddy. Once again, it added up. His disease and mine. He didn't live in an age when one said to friends, family, bosses: "I'm struggling with a problem and I need help."

I do.

I can.

PART II

Today

"Maybe you're wondering how I got here.
And maybe I am, too."

1976–1977

One morning in October 1976, as *Today*'s aging sunrise graphic lurched through its paces, I waited nervously while Tom Brokaw got business out of the way, then I said my little introductory piece, which began: "Maybe you're wondering how I got here. And maybe I am, too...."

Truer words I have never spoken. Was it supposed to be this quick, so unintentional? I was twenty-five and I hadn't waited my whole life for this, hadn't dreamed about it or ever said, "I'm going to be the next Barbara Walters!"

Just fourteen months earlier, I had been anchoring the news at noon in Indianapolis, when things started falling out of the blue—good and bad. At twenty-four, I'd been the first woman to anchor a weekday evening newscast in Chicago, and I was called, among other things, a "hood ornament" in the press. In New York, I was bracing for another media assault. But it didn't come. Instead I got sweet nothings, like "America's Sweetheart" or "Dawn's Early Sprite."

Since I was joining a program with a tradition of calling grown women "*Today* Girls," my age was not likely to cause offense. The "smart sorority girl" with the "cheerleader smile" was me—airbrushed. Overnight, my ordinary complexion was elevated to "flawless" and my dishwater-blond hair became a tastier honey-blond. There was universal agreement that one word was worth a thousand: *Midwestern*. Modifiers such as "fresh-faced" and "well-scrubbed" seemed redundant. *Time*'s variation on the theme was my favorite: "a corn-fed Catherine Deneuve."

There was a lot of media interest in me, especially because I was so young. Media coaching hadn't been invented yet. I felt totally on my own. After "What time do you get up?," the most common question I was asked was "What do you make?" I thought myself pretty clever when I quipped that I looked forward to the day when the same answer—three-thirty—covered both questions. Dr. Rolenzo A. Hanes, my retired orthodontist, saw his handiwork on the cover of the *Saturday Evening Post*. I was still wearing some of the hardware he had installed when I was a teenager; he wrote to suggest it was time to take it off.

My first month at the Dorset Hotel on West Fifty-fourth Street in New York, I ordered eggs Benedict from room service every night. Every morning, a car and a driver named Morty came to collect me. I did my hair every morning before I had my hair done again by Milton Buras. Bobbie Armstrong did my makeup, and Grace Cizignano was in charge of wardrobe; this was my first home in New York, and they were my new nuclear family.

Nobody proposed a makeover, and the only wardrobe advice—"Burn the dress!"—came from Tom Brokaw. At four-fifteen A.M., the city that never sleeps is barely stirring, and Rockefeller Plaza is still. The staff of the *Today* show was relaxed and friendly. I felt better already, more protected and supported than I had felt in Chicago.

At times I was a little too comfortable; I made mistakes—forgetting to put on the microphone, for instance. This also happened to Tom at least once. He started fishing around for the mike and when he discovered he was sitting on it, I ad–libbed, "You've got to keep the equipment warm." Not only is morning television forgiving, viewers tend to find imperfection endearing. When Tom and I had fun with our mistakes it made us look like real people, as the author Francine du Plessix Gray noted in a *Vogue* article, "Why I Love *Today*." I made the most mistakes, so I must have seemed the most real. My opening line—"Maybe you're wondering how I got here. And maybe I am, too"—set the bar as low as possible.

I literally felt more comfortable and more freely "myself" when I was on camera—possibly because I had to think more about *what* I was doing than about *how* I was doing. When I did a segment about diagnosing and treating high blood pressure, using a machine we had tested before the show, it turned out that my blood pressure was actually lower when we were on the air! Intuitively, I trusted the viewer to cut me some slack; I simply felt safe in the studio when the red light was on. When it went off, it was a different story; that's when I resumed my preoccupation with how I was doing. While nobody knew better than I did that Tom was Barbara Walters's successor, I was the one sitting in her office. All of my shortcomings were wrapped up in the instrument of torture that sat mute on my desk. I didn't merely inherit her job, I literally inherited her phone. In her hands, the telephone was a magic wand. Barbara had redefined the role of the woman on the *Today* show. She went on to become the acknowledged host of *Today* and the reigning queen of broadcast journalism. I did not inherit her title, but in a hundred ways I got the message that I should try to be more like her.

Jane is far less assertive than Walters, far more deferential to the men on the show. That is her nature.

—THE WASHINGTON POST, *Judy Bachrach, 1976*

Time would tell whether my deference was "my nature" or only a reflection of my stature. All the attention I was getting in the press was wildly disproportionate to my role on the show, which was really pretty insubstantial. I didn't even have a title until a reporter asked, and executive producer Paul Friedman pulled "regular member of the *Today* cast" right out of the air. "Absolutely," Paul told a newspaper reporter. "Absolutely she does not do as much as Brokaw. And will not. We made a decision that one person would be clearly in control and that person is Brokaw."

I knew how far Tom loomed above me, because standing in his shadow is where I felt safest. Any day, anything could happen. Mao's death was revealed the first day of my tryout—I found a quiet corner and stayed out of Tom's way. In my first month, the pope died—twice! And later Elvis and John Lennon. But I had nothing to fear while I was in Tom's protective shadow.

I craved Tom's approval, and also Paul Friedman's. Paul told me I got the job so someone on the staff would be younger than he was—thirty-one. My personal ratings meter was wired to Paul in the booth and Tom at the desk—my confidence rose and fell on their good opinion. And I didn't always have it. I didn't want to disappoint or get in trouble. As if trying to fire a rocket over my bow, Paul confided to *The Washington Post*, "I told her she needs to be more assertive and to contribute more ideas to the program." And he told still another reporter I should "read more books and weave them into [my] interviews." He told me the same thing during my semiannual performance evaluations. I regarded them as bad report cards, but made no effort to change; I just felt bad about myself. But perhaps I was more assertive than I was given credit for. One day, when I wasn't assigned a single interview in the course of the entire two-hour program, I called in to say that as my services wouldn't be required, I'd not be coming in!

After a year or two, I was doing nearly the same number of interviews as Tom did, though certainly not of equal importance, and when Tom was away, I filled in without a substitute. The company still considered me officially a "regular," but Paul told a reporter that most people thought of me as a co-host, and he did, too. By "most people," he meant *Today* viewers. I still felt most at home in the studio with viewers. But the paradox of my popularity was that my worst demographic was probably white males over forty-five—television executives. Speculation about my replacement began to appear in the press with some regularity.

As Mark Twain observed more than a hundred years ago, one's friends can often be counted upon to deliver bad news. I have a few samples of this because my father had a network of friends who clipped and mailed him anything—good or bad or horrible—that mentioned me. I had friends like that, too. One woke me up on a Saturday morning to say my successor had been named in the paper—had I seen it? My father wouldn't pass these clippings along to me directly, but I'd find them lying out on the coffee table when I went to visit. He wanted me to be prepared for the unexpected, not knowing I already was!

In 1977, Jann Wenner commissioned Frank Rich, then a film and television critic for *Time*, to write a profile of me for *Rolling Stone*, to coincide with my first anniversary on *Today*. My early success at twenty-five represented both a generational milestone and an aberration; I seemed so normal and my résumé was so short. Rich wrote, "How could a journalist who grew up in the sixties be so cheery and unaggressive? How could a young woman with a personality closer to Dinah Shore's than Lesley Stahl's rise so swiftly to the top of one of the most cutthroat professions in the country? It just doesn't make sense."

Jann Wenner never ran the story, but I was curious and asked Frank Rich to send me a courtesy copy about a year later. His questions were my questions, and I had no answers. American journalism, television and print, had just sharpened its knives on Watergate after a succession of national crises—civil rights, urban riots, assassinations, Vietnam. I seemed so out of sync with those times, which only deepened the mystery.

"What we all saw is an incredible ability to talk to the camera as if it were a person," Paul Friedman offered Rich as an explanation.

"Jane Pauley's 'Good morning' seems like a revelation. It may not seem like much of a talent—the talent to come across as warm and sincere and wholesome on television—but it is a talent few people have. Jane Pauley has it, and because she has it, she has enjoyed one of the most spectacularly accelerated careers in the history of television journalism."

Since I lacked a résumé, Rich went looking for a personality that might help explain the mystery of me. "If there's another Jane Pauley besides the one we see on TV, she's mighty hard to find," he wrote. Surveying my office, he found no clues: "The room contains no sign of personality at all." Then he went to Indiana and found my parents "as gracious as characters in a Norman Rockwell painting," "still in their Sunday best." My parents entertained their visitor in the living room, where most of the year even air didn't move. My father loved company.

My mother said I was "fairly serious." My father's observation, as quoted in the article, rang too true: "Janie dated, but she didn't talk on the phone much and seldom brought her date in when she came home; when he dropped her at the door that was the end of it." Missing the reference to another Jane Pauley—one called "Janie"—Rich concluded the interview with a tour of the bedroom I hadn't occupied in eight years, finding no clues to my existence "extant."

Rich wrote, "Perhaps someday she will grow old, and, in an industry that has little use for older women, she could be in real trouble. But in the meantime, there are far worse ways to wake up than by looking at Jane Pauley. Smart, beautiful, sturdy, self-made and unfailingly pleasant, she really is the daughter that Americans love to dream about and, except on television, never find."

So "wholesome and Midwestern," my sister told him. "We spend a lot of time trying to live that down."

And Rich concluded: "Jane Pauley's Midwestern upbringing was so placid and so conventional it was impossible to overcome."

There was an explanation for our upbringing. By the time I read Rich's article, in 1978, my sister and I were beginning to understand that it had been far less conventional than it looked, and that it had been "placid" for a reason.

There are more of our kind than any other bird in the forest. Yet the rapid accumulation of change is not always progress, and forward motion is not always an advance.

— THE BEAK OF THE FINCH, *by Jonathan Weiner*

I happened to be reading *The Beak of the Finch* at the same time I was rereading Frank Rich's article about my early years with NBC.

Weiner writes about watching natural selection at work among the finches of the Galápagos; one finch is favored during a drought, while another succeeds under flood conditions. The variation is a barely observable but measurable difference in the size and shape of a bird's beak.

In 1976, lacking perspective on the cultural landscape, nobody could have seen the changes that favored a Dinah Shore type over a Lesley Stahl type. Watergate was over, the war was over, and the country was suffering a "national malaise." In the darkness before "Morning in America," maybe the country was likely to find appealing an "unaggressive," wholesome girl who seemed bright but put on no airs.

I was the right bird.

PART III

Yesterday

The house I grew up in had twin dormers on the roof. They looked like eyes. If the shades were pulled, it was sleeping; if one was pulled and the other not, it seemed to be winking. If the little house could talk, it wouldn't have more to tell than I would. The "secrets" were so well hidden from my sister, Ann, and me that there was no need for locked doors or even closed doors. We could poke around any drawer in the house. Daddy's suitcase was perpetually lying open on the bed as he was coming or going—there was nothing off-limits. I can take a mental tour of every cranny in the house even now. This openness was not an illusion; the greater significance lay in what, and especially who, wasn't there.

1996

In 1996, NBC News sent its anchors fanning out across the country—Katie and Ann, Matt and Al, and Brian, Stone, and me—to the Pacific coast, the Plains, suburban New York City, Virginia, Brooklyn, Buffalo, each to do a story about the place he or she came from. The series was called "Going Home." I panicked a little at the prospect. My first thought, irrational as it sounds, was *But nothing happened there.*

I found a story, and not just a story but one that took me to my own front yard. It was about a federal busing order that brought racial diversity to my old high school. The opening shot would show me waiting for a school bus on the porch of the house where I grew up and where I had waited for many school buses myself. But in fact, I hadn't found one story, I had found two, and the second one, I can say without exaggeration, would change me forever.

While I was waiting for the crew to set up the shot, the current owner of the house graciously let me come inside and take a look around. I had been thirteen when we moved away. I was forty-five when I came back. My mother had been gone less than a year and my father had passed away three years before that, but for me their presence in that house was still palpable—the doorknobs they'd turned, their closets, Mom's kitchen sink, the paneled walls in the basement. I believe they had decided it was time to move when Daddy ran out of walls to panel. Touching the heads of nails I might have handed him seemed to open a portal into a long-forgotten place.

I went upstairs to their bedroom. There was the dormer window that looked out onto the street. I remembered Daddy balanced outside it on one end of a board he had laid across the windowsill, stationing Mommy on the other end to keep the board secure while he stood outside and painted the house. It amused him to think that she might hear the phone ring and leap up, sending him flying over the house like a Wallenda. He was a funny guy.

As I went through room after room, peeking in a few closets and expecting to find our clothes and our sheets and towels organized exactly as I could still see them in my mind's eye, I wasn't bracing for any bad memories, only aching with the wish that I might find "us" still living there.

Three years later, there was a second series, this time called "Roots." The assignment for NBC News anchors was to tell a story about our ancestors. I seemed to be the only one who had difficulty finding a story. Fatefully, I decided to go back just one generation and tell a story about my father, showing how his life was intertwined with the great events of the first half of the twentieth century. Tom Brokaw had not yet written *The Greatest Generation*, but that was the idea I was going for. If "Going Home" in 1996 had set me up, then "Roots" knocked me down. For weeks, I gathered pictures and documents and old newspaper clippings from family and friends, along with the odd assemblage that passed for our family archives.

It was an immersion in old memories plus new discoveries. For forty-nine years, a box of letters, hundreds of them, had sat undisturbed in the houses and condos where my parents had lived. I started to read them for the first time.

My father's entire early life was punctuated with loss and trauma, as I said in the *Dateline* story that aired in March 1999. Months later, sitting on the floor, surrounded by all those letters and pictures and newspaper clippings, I happened to notice the date on Daddy's father's obituary—January 1940—and I thought, *That's wrong!* I had reported that my grandfather died of leukemia three years earlier. It took me a few minutes to absorb the magnitude of my father's loss. My father hadn't lost his parents three years apart as I had reported—it was only three months apart. His mother was killed in April 1940, in an automobile accident. The car slammed into a tree. Daddy was driving. His parents were fifty-two, and he, only twenty-three.

In an 8-mm film of a road trip he took in the summer of 1941 with his best buddies, Daddy appeared fully recovered. They went to Mexico and back by way of Los Angeles, Big Sur, Salt Lake City, and Mount Rushmore—and all in ten days! "Making good time" was my father's lifelong mantra.

Daddy had turned down a full scholarship to college after graduating at the top of his class (of sixteen) from Morristown (Indiana) High School. He invested in a business course instead—typing and stenography. But I don't think this made the nascent list of his "disappointments." While I see a lot of Dick Pauley in Jimmy Stewart's George Bailey in *It's a Wonderful Life* (they even looked alike), staking his chances on a college education wasn't part of his life's plan. It wasn't part of the culture of my native Indiana. Instead of college, a cousin remembers, Daddy wanted "to get productive right away," which sounds on the money. Even the phrase "on the money" sounds on the money. Hard cash was the only money Daddy trusted from age eleven, after the stock market crashed and took with it the family business and his father's dream of a chain of Pauley variety stores.

Getting productive right away was part of his temperament.

If it's possible to lose yourself in a war, Daddy had the opportunity to do so. At twenty-four, he left with a busload of fellow draftees three weeks before the attack on Pearl Harbor on December 7, 1941. He was married in uniform, on Christmas Day 1943, thirty years to the day after his parents were married. Heading home on a troopship at Christmas 1945 through a late-season hurricane, he wasn't making good time. But within three months, he thirty and my mother thirty-one, they were making up for lost time—she was pregnant. Before Christmas of 1946, Daddy had buried his firstborn child, a boy, strangled at birth by the umbilical cord.

Daddy returned to the hospital with a gift for my mother—a pair of lamps—and reassuring promises that she'd be back in that maternity dress in no time! My sister, Ann, was born thirteen months later, in 1948.

Ann Elizabeth was the answer to Daddy's prayers, or as nearly so as a baby girl could possibly be. His "little doll" was breathtaking, but very early Daddy noticed and nurtured a far more precious asset. No one would remember my first sentence or when I spoke it, but here is Ann's: "Mommy, get me my Taylor-Tot [stroller]; I want to take my dolly for a ride." A compound sentence! Soon after, Daddy began to teach her " 'Twas the Night Before Christmas," which she memorized before she was two.

"I have worried whether all our sorrows would affect you or the baby. I know they say it doesn't affect the baby but I still wonder. I have had untold heartaches, hon, but I don't suppose it has hurt me."

1950

I was born at an inopportune moment. My parents had settled into their postwar lives and had picked a house for a family of three plus one more due in the fall—me. The last thing anyone thought would happen after World War II was another war. So when hostilities broke out in Korea in the summer of 1950, the country was ill prepared for it and turned, by necessity, to reservists. Many were married men with kids, as my father was. It was a devastating blow, this abrupt change in my parents' plans. Overnight, the happy anticipation of my arrival was nullified by dread over his departure. A new baby was a further complication.

My mother was eight months pregnant with me when they said good-bye. They wrote letters to each other almost every day for the next ten months: "I've gotten myself into a terrible mess, Honey." My father bitterly regretted his decision to take inactive reserve status instead of a discharge after World War II. For a few extra dollars a month, he had put his little family in a terrible predicament.

"I've just heard MacArthur has asked for unconditional surrender. These are rough terms and it may mean opening guns. We must pray, Honey. Maybe we

are selfish to want to end the Korean affair knowing the North Koreans could always be a threat, but I just want to come home so badly."

After basic training he was transferred about a thousand miles closer to Korea, to a base near San Francisco, from which troops were being deployed to the Far East. He tried to prepare himself mentally to go, while praying to be sent home. There were reports about a new point system that would determine when and in what order the reservists would be discharged. *Newsweek* reported that reservists with four dependents would be discharged, but baby only made three dependents. Furthermore, I wouldn't make the cutoff date—September 30. But I redeemed myself in the eleventh hour.

My parents had opposing blood types—he was Rh–negative and she was Rh–positive. If my blood type was negative, there was a risk that her blood would attack mine. This was a lucky break, because it enabled the Red Cross to work a small miracle and persuade the army that the danger warranted the presence of the father. Daddy got a ticket home. "Our little furlough promoter," he called me.

In letters, his preparations for coming home are almost comical—plans and contingency plans go on for two pages. But by the time his letter arrived, so had I—almost two weeks early. It was just a three-week furlough, but family lore has it that thanks to me, he missed a troopship heading to the Far East. A buddy wrote a farewell note, ending, "Take care of that new girl."

I was born on Halloween and looked a little scary. I had some unspecified "condition." My mother caught Daddy measuring my face to see how off my ears, eyes, and nose were. "Maybe she'll be pretty when she gets some teeth and hair," he wrote later, sounding none too hopeful. Three months after that, he checked on my progress: "How much does little Janie weigh? I don't suppose there's any evidence of hair?" My mother answered: "She weighs about 12 pounds and has no more hair than when you were here."

At thirty-four, Master Sergeant Pauley was the second-oldest out of 218 men taking basic training at Fort Hood. At the start of basic, some of the younger guys had their doubts the "old man" would make it.

My father was a paradox. He didn't look hale and hearty, but his constitution was strong. In fact, he boasted a little in another letter home that he finished the infiltration course sixth or seventh out of thirty-five, creeping over barbed wire and under a barrage of machine-gun fire. "I can double time with rifle, bayonet, canteen & helmet and survive as good as anyone," he wrote. My father was not a macho man; he was an evaporated-milk salesman for the Wilson Milk Company. His letters make it painfully clear that he acted one way:

I don't complain to the men. They can't understand how I can keep such an even temper. They just don't know I get burnt up the same as they do. One more thing. This morning at reveille formation my platoon gave me a Schaefer Pen & Pencil set. I was really appreciative but embarrassed. This is not a common thing to do, they having known me only 3 weeks. So, hon, even bad conditions often times furnish their fine moments.

And felt another:

I'm a little blue tonight, hon! My letter will show it, I suspect. But I'll get over it—probably by morning. That's one good thing about sleeping—even when you have the blues when you go to sleep, you don't have them while you're sleeping.

I felt a little blue, off and on this morning, knowing that I wouldn't have mail today, but I "outgrew" it and have felt pretty fair the rest of the day—for Monday.

"It hurt so much hearing you cry the night I called. I had to have a cry too, hon. I get a lump in my throat so many times, then when I'm in bed I generally get it off my chest and feel relaxed. I just can't look at that little doll's picture without it hurting so bad."

In nearly all of Daddy's letters, there's an update: The blues are pretty bad, not as bad as Sunday, and so on. But he and my mother were both depressed. Their daily letters were a lifeline. But just as Daddy didn't complain to the men in his platoon, my mother didn't complain to him, though between the lines, she suffers as much—or more. Isolated with her worries and two little girls, she tries to be upbeat. She wrote that she learned patience from long winter days, and that she was learning how to improve her outlook.

I was a low-maintenance baby, the right baby for a woman whose nerves were on edge. Mom wrote to Daddy that I was her "ray of sunshine." I not only slept through the night, but I went to sleep without fussing and was so full of smiles that when she fed me, sometimes I forgot to swallow because I was smiling at her. It made my father sad to think about what he was missing.

"It's certainly a blessing that little doll Janie is so good. Gosh, Hon, I've thought many times how I'm missing rocking her to sleep and it hurts. I'm not going to know her like I did Ann. And she's not going to know Daddy. It's a cruel world but we must count our blessings and be thankful."

My mother replied with comforting assurances—and a caution:

"Kiddies are fickle. They think whoever is looking after them is their mama. Mothers think they know them . . . but they don't. In three days you'll know her and she'll know you."

But don't think about rocking her; she doesn't respond to being held and is cutest when let lay in her bassinet.

My mother was her father's daughter. Fred Patterson was a member of a clan of quiet people. They were famous for having a keen sense of hearing and for not talking much unless it was to say something funny. It was said that a dozen Pattersons could sit together in the parlor and not obscure the sound of a ticking clock.

Fred Patterson's resemblance to Abraham Lincoln—he had high sunken cheekbones and deep-set eyes—caused permanent confusion in my formative brain, because I met my grandfather first and subsequently recognized Lincoln's resemblance to him, not vice versa. His lanky stride in work boots and overalls—which seemed about a hundred years old—the image of an ax in his hand (for chicken dinners), and the timeless context of rural Indiana only underscored my conviction that they were one man, somehow.

My grandfather was vulnerable to depression. He kept a daily journal, in which he noted the weather, who drove by, and how many eggs were sold and pigs born. There are also blank pages for months at a time.

My grandparents met in a church choir. Fred Patterson lived with his mother and worked in the accounting department of a canning factory. He was a champion at ciphering contests when he could barely reach the blackboard. My grandmother Edna Mae Bradford was a nurse, having commuted weekly, by bicycle, to nursing school in Indianapolis—a twenty-mile trip. But when they "went to housekeeping," they bought a farm.

Edna Mae Bradford had been an only child and was evidently comfortable making decisions—big ones. First she decided that her husband's mother should live with one of the other Patterson siblings; second, that his office was not a healthy environment—

one of his sisters had died of tuberculosis. My grandfather entered into marriage an accountant and emerged a farmer.

My mother, like her father, loved doing figures. She too entered into marriage an accountant, but she emerged a homemaker. In her high school yearbook, Mary Patterson was officially remembered by her Franklin High School graduating class of 1933 for "being quiet." Her report card had straight A's, but her dance card was blank. Unlike her popular older sister, Martha, who has the personality of Eve Arden, and her younger sister, Eleanor, who looked like Donna Reed, she never had a boyfriend. Mary spent her childhood at the piano, practicing as much as five hours a day. My grandmother's rule was lessons before chores, according to Aunt Martha, who admits she would have preferred chores before lessons. I can imagine my grandmother calculating that studying and practicing piano were a better investment of Mary's time than cooking and chores. My mother's dream job, according to her senior–class will, was to be a missionary or a homemaker. But getting married was not a foregone conclusion. She'd need a job. She enrolled in the same business school my father would attend.

When I was growing up, we had a collection of fantastic 1930s sheet music in our piano bench that was never accounted for, in part because I never asked. It was a surprise to discover that my mother had played part-time at a supper club. But her day job was at the Wilson Milk Company: Those fingers were as adept at a typewriter as at a piano, and she was a virtuoso on the Comptometer, a type of adding machine. She might have liked her job as an accounts payable clerk, even if she made only seven dollars a week! She might even have loved her job once that new boy arrived: Taylor Wilson's executive secretary, Richard Pauley. She confided to her sisters that she had met "the man she was going to marry." But the sisters exchanged "looks"—at that point he hadn't even asked Mary for a date.

Keeping busy seemed to be my parents' shared coping strategy—and a productive one. But coping isn't healing. When the whole bad business of war was finally over, they did what hard times had trained them to do—they just got on with their lives. My parents had many reasons for not looking back.

If my mother played her piano for diversion, I have no memory of it. It was a quiet house. No phone ringing. No one knocking at the door. No TV. But I can imagine her craning to hear the paperboy, waiting with dread and anticipation to see the war news. She might have paused to make a cup of instant coffee—with a splash of Wilson's milk: no sugar; read the paper. The news from the war might have come in dispatches twice a day...and then she'd sit down to write a letter to Dick, often offering her analysis. My father sent a loving admonition that her obsessive attention to radio newscasts was unhealthy.

She was the defender of the domain. She wasn't just holding down the fort; she had the house built, under her own supervision, when he was away. And then she defended that fortress against the indefensible—the unexpected bad news that would creep in under the door and take her dreams away.

My father came home in the summer of 1951, when I was ten months old. The army was one bad memory he wore like a badge. He kept the army boots for lawn mowing—Lord knows they were broken in!—and wore his wool olive-drab sweater for twenty years. Not out of affection, but to amortize the year of his life the "Korean mess" took from him, from *us*. I grew up knowing the sad Korea story, but I liked the happy ending—the part where I kept Daddy from getting on the boat.

My mother's observation that I didn't respond to being held like other babies was contradicted by my later reputation as a lap child. I must have soaked up his attention like a sponge. One of my earliest memories involves Daddy trying unsuccessfully to put me in the nursery at church, while I clung to him like a bad monkey that wouldn't let go. I loved being held by anybody. But I don't suppose my mother relented and let him rock me to sleep.

Daddy had been a stranger to me when he came home, I suppose, but I soon considered him the life of the family. He took us to Linder's for ice cream when we least expected it. He had funny words for things—like *si-foddlin,* which meant "crooked." He read the stories, heard our prayers, and tucked us in. He brought the Christmas tree, put up the lights, and made fudge for our stockings. He made breakfast for dinner when it was Mom's night off on Sunday.

But he was gone about a third of the time, even after he came home from the army. As a salesman, he spent three or four nights a week on the road. Perhaps he was right to worry I might never know my daddy.

The fundamental construct of my family is that we were always two sets of pairs. Mommy and Daddy were a pair. Mommy and I were a pair. And Ann and Daddy were another. Ann and I were a pair, too, but we were very different. She got a doll when I came home from the hospital, but she wasn't the kind of girl who played with dolls a lot. My dolls suffered all kinds of indignities: They quickly lost all their clothes, limbs, hair, and sometimes their heads.

Our house was among the first on the block, and Daddy worried that my sister's lack of playmates might make her "backward," but Ann had me. When Mom put my crib in Ann's room—thereafter *our* room—Ann wasn't scared at night anymore. That's when we formed an elite club with only two members. It was Mom who was so alone.

When Ann went to nursery school, it must have been a very quiet house. My mother didn't mind not talking for long stretches. Taking the bus downtown with her was the height of adventure for me, even if it meant an hour picking out fabric and thread and zippers and buttons when I wasn't even eye-level with the counter.

When my sister finally found somebody to play with other than me, it was Richard Warren. He had something of a reputation as the neighborhood tough when he was five or six. Once he made a move for the tricycle my cousin Mindy was riding, and she bit him. Another time he ran off with Ann's shoe, but she caught him and beat him up with it. I followed Ann across the street, but I played inside, with Richard's mother, Norma, my first best friend.

Norma was on the young side of postwar baby-boom mothers and was still pretty. By young, I mean younger than my mother, who was already over forty by then. Norma was probably still in her twenties. She and I played house. I took for granted my company was a delight and made her housework fun. My favorite part of our visits was laundry. Her washing machine stood on four tall legs and seemed to dance. The best part was watching her pull each piece of clothing out of the tub and run it through the wringer—a contraption far more fascinating than the plain white box in our basement.

Norma was also lucky—she could drive. Our garage was empty during the week when Daddy was on the road, but he must have built a two-car garage in the expectation that Mom would learn to drive, too. And she did. We cowered on the floor, squealing, when Daddy let her practice with us in the car. But pretty soon, a vintage 1940s Plymouth was parked on the right side of the garage.

There's a picture of me sitting alone on the steps of our house. Daddy's patience had finally been rewarded. Janie had teeth and hair.

My identity was organized around the proposition that I was the delightful little girl whose mouth is wide open and eyes are tight shut in most family photographs. Though I wasn't exactly pretty, I was more invested in being cute.

It was not a delightful little girl but a shy little sister who went with Ann to meet the new family in the new house next door—the Falconburys. I didn't take my eyes off the green carpet during that first visit, the first of thousands. They had two boys— and a little girl! She became my second best friend; her name was Donna. She had mischievous dark eyes that matched her auburn hair. Soon a little chink was carved out of the hedge between our houses at the point that was the shortest distance between my back door and her front porch.

Next door to Donna is where Carol Morrow lived. Carol was a quiet, thoughtful little girl who would pack a book to read in the morning when she came for a sleepover. Her favorite words were "let's make," and her mother had an endless supply of round Quaker Oatmeal containers to make things from. Carol once wrote a book the size of a postage stamp. Donna and Carol each had a brother named Rick, but they were very different. Carol's brother introduced stamp collecting to the neighborhood; Donna's introduced red dog poker.

Diversity in our fifties neighborhood meant that Presbyterians, Baptists, and Methodists could live side by side. The Morrows were Methodists. The Falconburys were Baptists. We were Presbyterians. Sometimes I went to church with Donna on Sunday evenings, and I noticed that Baptists were more emotional than Presbyterians. Not only did people never cry in our church, but Ann and I were often overcome with giggles. In Donna's church, there was quite a lot of talk of Satan and hell. Donna's mother, Jane Falconbury, must have found something so peaceful at church that it sustained her the whole week long. Jane was unfailingly serene in a house that was always simmering—and sometimes bursting into a full boil, like the time Donna's oldest brother, Tom, chased Rick around the yard with a hammer. Jane carried herself with grace even when she was sitting in the cab of a pickup truck (which Donna found mortifying). She was forever vacuuming a few more threads from that green carpet or running to the store for a gallon of milk, sometimes at eleven at night, and she would be up making hot breakfasts the next morning. No sooner did she get the boys out of the house and into school than she started a nursery school in her living room for all the little kids left on the block. I loved Jane's school so much that I couldn't wait for the clock on the top of the TV to say it was time, so I helped the big hand go a little faster. I was never that anxious to go to school again.

Once when I was home sick, Jane appeared at the back door. She must have been baking that day, and she had a little extra pie dough and some filling, which she put in an empty frozen potpie tin. It was a little tiny replica of a pumpkin pie. I didn't care much for pumpkin pie, but I loved tiny replicas of anything. And she had made it just for me. I would never forget it, nor would I ever live up to the standard she set for loving and caring for a family that, it seemed to me, took its treasure for granted.

My undirected writing style, "finding out what my fingers know," was not invented by me. The process is usually described as "top of the mind"—when a channel to the unconscious opens and reveals itself on the page. I can't do it at will, which explains why I've been at it so long. But the more I write, the more I think it's not at all arbitrary which childhood impressions and recollections the unconscious mind clings to.

It made sense that I would write about my first actual best friends, Donna Falconbury and Carol Morrow, but the impulse to write about Donna's mother came from a less predictable place. I wrote about Jane Falconbury's little pie years ago. Finally I decided it had no real place in the story. No more than twenty minutes later, the backroom guys shot a message over the transom. The idea that came to me was that the unconscious meaning was embedded in the phrase "took its treasure for granted." The significance of the story is that a person might deserve, or need, more loving attention than she got. And that her name could be Jane. Or Janie. Or Mary.

In Sunday school, the littlest ones sat in front on tiny chairs, and we sang a strange song about rolling our burdens away. I imagined rocks rolling down a hill, having no idea what burdens were. Later, when I joined the grown-up congregation, we sang hymns about burdens, giving them to Jesus, along with cares and woe. Ideas were taking shape in me now. I was old enough to understand that feelings like heartache and worry could be heavy things that you carried in your heart. You couldn't load them up like gravel in Daddy's wheelbarrow and cart them away. Jesus, evidently, was ready to help carry those burdens. Daddy never knew it, but I was trying to help carry a few of his, too.

I sensed there were heavy things on my father's heart, despite his gentle countenance and cheerful disposition. He was a man with two sides. His public face was the father I knew. The private face was the invisible pull he had on everyone who loved him, the face I knew about intuitively. Here's a paradox: I knew so much about this as a child and so little as an adult.

If I was precocious in any way, it was in my ability to discern that even though my father was outgoing, energetic, competent, and very popular, he projected a vulnerability so palpable that even a little girl understood it, long before she could define it.

Maybe it was his onlyness—being the only man in our house, an only child, the only one of them left.

Daddy emptied his pockets onto the top of the bureau. I thought of it as the bank of Daddy. It was my understanding that I could make small withdrawals without asking. I left the peppermints—Daddy was never without them.

His suits hung in the closet, his robe on a hook on the door. Wingtips on the floor. He wore suspenders, no belt. His closet smelled like leather and shoe polish. Mom's smelled like play clothes. Her shoes for every day, Sunday pumps, and a pair of red pumps I played dress-up in lay on the floor amidst the jumble of our dirty clothes.

Daddy had a dignity that was often remarked upon—a courtly demeanor people found admirable, not off-putting. Daddy was most at home in a suit and tie, which he wore six days of seven, counting church. With a gray fedora, he looked real sharp. He didn't look quite right in casual clothes—he looked like a soldier in his civvies on a three-day pass. I was often told that my father was "such a gentleman," and nothing about the man I knew at home contradicted that.

He never swore. He never shouted. I never heard him speak a sharp word to my mother—or to anyone else. But I never knew what to make of one incident.

No family reunion was complete without a re-creation of my cousin Mindy earnestly informing the rest of us—in a dead-serious whisper—that we were to dine in..."a bar!" While I'd never seen an actual bar before, Miss Kitty ran one that Marshal Dillon frequented on *Gunsmoke*, so I wasn't appalled by the environment. As for liquor, the strongest thing I'd ever seen my parents drink was coffee.

The establishment turned out to be a hybrid—part road-house and part family restaurant. It was still daylight when we were heading back to the parking lot; something got my attention, and I turned around in time to see two men seem to tumble out the door—and one of them was Daddy!

It seemed like my Uncle Henry had him by the throat! Were they fooling around? Daddy was no fighter, but there was one thing I'd seen him fight for—and that was the check! It was such a fetish with him, always grabbing the check. I know Mom sometimes wanted to throttle him, and maybe this time Uncle Henry did. In any event, Mindy was right—bars were bad news. I never knew what to do with that bad memory and the bad feeling that came with it.

Daddy rarely called home when he was on the road (long-distance cost money—"it's our nickel"), so I didn't worry: out of sight, out of mind. But if he was in the range of, say, forty minutes, he'd make the local call to give Mom his ETA. Then I'd keep an eye on the clock. What a relief to hear the crunch of gravel in the driveway, and the slam of the car door—just to make sure. I probably beat Mom to the door for our hugs.

My mother needed a quiet house to soothe her jangled nerves. The hum of a sewing machine—*zzzzzip*, stop, *zzzzzip*, stop—meant that her mind was at work on something other than her troubles.

My mother was most content when her mind was occupied with a task, and sewing took a lot of concentration. Mom made most of our clothes. The sound of her sewing machine meant she was "getting a lot done," which was her equivalent of Daddy's "making good time." It defined a good day. It was a barometer of her mood. When she had "one of my lazy days," it was not a good day. But my mother was never really lazy; she was depressed.

Daddy believed that a man's self-respect floated with his finances. One didn't need to be "rich," just not "a bum." Not coincidentally, his spirits tanked whenever the company "disappointed" him, as when he was drafted again and the company cut off his salary. But as soon as he was discharged he went straight back there, filing his hurt and anger under "that Korean mess"—and he stayed at the company for the rest of his working life. Dick Pauley and the Wilson Milk Company were one.

After their marriage, as was the custom at the time, Mom had quit working, but she retained her status as a peer at the office for years afterward. She was smart, she knew the players, she knew the history; she was a silent partner. He was the titular head of the household by virtue of prevailing custom and his name being on the paycheck, but his majority was as slim as 51 percent of the voting shares.

My mother was not the quintessential fifties housewife. Her personality and public persona were completely at odds. She looked like "the little woman," but she was pretty big at home. Though this notion would never have crossed her mind, she did not make being a homemaker her identity. What she probably thought about while doing the laundry was Daddy's work.

My mother's aspiration to be a missionary or homemaker was surely inspired by her own mother's example. My grandmother would have been a hard act for anyone to follow. A missionary/homemaker would be a pretty fair description of her. She was a leader who served. In snapshots she appears to be hiding her hands. Milking, hoeing, weeding, cooking, washing, collecting eggs, mending—everything a farmwife had to do in an average day was done with her hands. She watered her immense garden in back of the garage with a watering can filled at the pump in front of the garage. She didn't have indoor plumbing until after the war.

My grandmother had been the daughter of an alcoholic. Despite the chaos of her home life, my grandmother managed to get a high school education. The hospital she chose for nursing school was a psychiatric hospital for the treatment of "nervous" disorders, including alcoholism. I'm impressed that she didn't run from her past; she ran toward it.

There's a picture of a typical weekend at my grandparents' farm. It's after dark, my grandmother's gray hair is braided and twisted under a hairnet, she wears an apron, her hands are deep in a sink of dirty dishes. The back of a fashionably coiffed head appears in the lower right foreground—watching. It's my Aunt Eleanor. My mother and Aunt Martha are out of the picture, but they're sitting at the kitchen table, too, watching Mama work. She would have it no other way.

She had not raised her daughters for a life of hard work from sunup to past dark, but she chose it. My mother did not inherit (nor did I) her mother's robust health and stamina. Her heart may have been damaged by a childhood bout of scarlet fever. Her most notable contribution to the family fortunes had been a business idea—they should grow tomatoes and sell them to the canning plant. I'm sure she did the math.

PART IV

Janie

My father had a nickname for me: Pain. I never thought about the implications of being called Pain my whole life; it was just a term of endearment, not the least bit odd. Only my father called me Pain and that was the only thing he called me. I was named Margaret Jane in honor of his mother, Margaret Grandison. The Margaret was silent except for second grade, when I was too shy to say my name: Janie.

Eastridge Elementary School

For two years I stood at the picture window and watched the big kids collect in front of our house on East New York Street early every morning, sometimes standing in the dark or huddled in the rain.

Even though everybody was waiting for it, when the big yellow bus turned right off Post Road, lit up like a spaceship, it always seemed so sudden. And then just as suddenly, with a salute of folding doors, it carried off most of the neighborhood.

One day the school bus came around the corner and I was swallowed up and carried away, too! What a disappointment when I realized I was not going to learn to read the first day. What was worse, I didn't notice the number of the bus that took me to school—I didn't know there'd be twenty just like it at the end of the day. I picked one. At the end of his run, the bus driver noticed a little girl where a little girl shouldn't be and took me home. Mommy was waiting at the front porch. I guess I knew my address.

Nineteen fifty-six was the shakedown cruise at Eastridge Elementary School. The red bricks were the only concession to the schoolhouse of yore; our modern, one-story version clung as close to the ground as a suburban ranch house. We first graders, born four to five years after World War II, occupied three jam-packed classrooms at the far end of the building, forty-some to a class. I was the youngest in the class.

My room was closest to the exit, but farthest from everything else. Sometimes the "walk, don't run" rule could stretch the distance to the bathroom from painfully to impossibly far. Then a kindly gray-haired gentleman in a gray jumpsuit, whose name was Mr. Rigney, would be summoned with his sawdust and rag mop, which he steered about in a large silver bucket on wheels. Such an accident happened to me only once, when the teacher's "take one bite" rule bit back. I gagged on a green bean and my whole lunch hit the floor—I "tossed my cookies," in my father's exceptional phrase. So the patient Mr. Rigney and his bucket brigade appeared, followed after a short while by my mother, who drove me home in her secondhand Plymouth the color of overcooked green beans.

In my five-year-old imagination, Mr. Cox, the school principal, was the Wizard of Oz (the great and terrible) in a suit and tie. Stiff and stern, he walked as if he didn't have joints, and wore a perpetually blank expression (were his eyes actually in the back of his head?). With a look, he could freeze a herd of thundering hall-runners in the tracks of their Red Ball Jets. My strategy was to be invisible in the presence of grown-ups: Obey rules, shrink into my shoes, and blend into the brick wall behind my red plaid dress. The irony: The tough kids weren't intimidated, but the timid kids were.

The first day the new cafeteria opened at Eastridge Elementary School, a rumor swept the hungry first graders lining up outside: bean soup. Bean soup? The prospect of facing a bowl of some-

My maternal grandmother,
Edna Bradford, later Patterson.

My paternal grandmother,
Margaret Grandison, later Pauley.

My father with his parents,
Albert and Margaret Pauley.

My maternal grandparents,
Edna Bradford Patterson and Fred Patterson.

My parents, Richard G. Pauley and Mary Patterson Pauley.

My parents on their wedding day, December 25, 1943.

Daddy and one of the Andrews Sisters overseas during the war.

Daddy on a troopship, coming home from World War II.

The Pauley family in front of our house,
the summer after Daddy returned home from the war.

My sister, Ann.

*That's me, just under a year old,
with a promotional display from Wilson's Milk,
the business my father worked for.*

Ann and me at Lake Michigan.

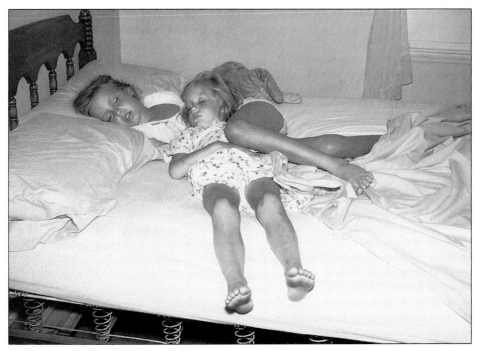

Ann, with her head on the pillow, and me.

*Just before I turned three, at Ann's graduation
from kindergarten. My grandmother made
the dress I'm wearing.*

Me, at age three, on the steps of our house in Indianapolis. Daddy built the garage.

The Pauley family at home. I'm sitting on my mother's lap;
Ann sits next to Daddy.

Ann and me in Sarasota, Florida.

Sitting with Ann and our cousins, Tom Davidson and Melinda Scott Miller, in a wheelbarrow pushed by my father at our maternal grandparents' farm.

Me, with Poofadiddle, and Ann, with Flippy, wearing outfits our mother made.

My grandmother at the farm.

My first-grade school picture. Mom cut my hair.

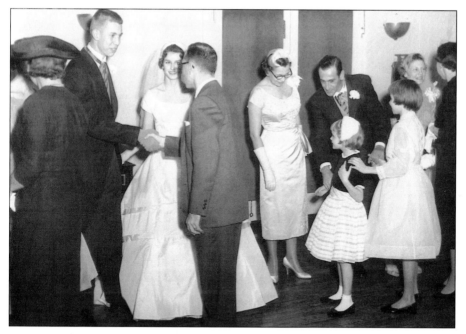

*Ann and me at the wedding of a family friend, wearing dresses our mother made.
Ann puts her hand on my shoulder . . .*

. . . and I reach back.

I'm second from the right, and Donna Falconbury is at the far right, on the cheerleading squad in sixth grade.

As governor of Girls' State.

HOOSIER GIRLS' STATE, INC.

INDIANA UNIVERSITY

American Legion Auxiliary　　　　　　**Department of Indiana**

MISS JANE PAULEY

1967 Governor Hoosier Girls' State

TUESDAY, JUNE 25, 1968

At Girls Nation with Secretary of State Dean Rusk.

*With the National Forensic League speech team
at Warren Central High School. I'm in the middle,
with long hair.*

In college, "cooking" with
Marty Youngquist (middle) and Judy Smith Abbett.

thing I'd never even heard of was too terrible to bear. I wanted to go home! My mother came to get me. She must have made a stop on the way. Soon, I was sitting in my place at the kitchen table, waiting for her to give me lunch—a bowl of bean soup!

Wanting to go home was a natural response to stress, but as my cagey mother tried to teach me, it's not always the best response. I learned the wrong lesson: I like bean soup.

I learned a new word: *burglar*. A burglar was a someone, not a something, who would sneak into houses at night and steal things. Unfortunately, it was nighttime when the topic came up in conversation, while I stood in the backseat of the car, my face between my parents' shoulders, all of us staring at the deepest darkness on the other side of the headlight's beam. There were things out there that I now understood were beyond my father's control. We should lock the doors against them right now here in the car, but what would happen when we got to New York Street and turned right off Post Road, and into the driveway, where the garage door was almost always open? What burglar wanted an oily old lawn mower, a rake with a prong poking out, drippy cans with lids that had to be pried off with a screwdriver, or my bike or skates? Who cared about that stuff?—a burglar could take it all—just let him not be there when we pull in!

Daddy had an elderly aunt who left a helpful note: "The key is under the mat"—even I knew that was so silly. But seen in this new light, I understood why you'd lock the door and want to *hide* the key! Did burglars ever need keys? So now, even as the key turned, and forever after that—was someone on the other side of the door lurking in the dark? Could nothing be done? Was everyone powerless to stop them?

What I really didn't get about this new idea of outlaws: Why didn't their mothers put a stop to it? I also wondered about motorcycle gangs—how sad and foolish they were going to look when they got old. I was convinced they'd act like normal people and stop being highway pirates if they thought about their future grandchildren. Meanwhile, Daddy practically lived on the highway. We took all our vacations in the company car. How could I relax anymore, when he took his little nap beside the road? Or even when he woke up and we had Pepsis and bologna sandwiches? A mommy, a sleeping daddy, and two little girls— what tempting targets.

To this day, I'm scared of motorcycles in groups of three or more—even when they ride with granny geezers in the sidecar. And at nighttime it only needs to be one—a biker so bad he doesn't even have Hell's Angels for friends!

Tucking us in at night was Daddy's special job. He heard our prayers: "Now I lay me down to sleep I pray the Lord my soul to keep. If I should die before I wake I pray the Lord my soul to take." I think for Daddy it was like an insurance policy that I wouldn't up and die in the night, because when you named your fears, they wouldn't happen; or if they did, at least you would deprive them of the satisfaction of taking you by surprise. I knew Daddy worked it out like that—so did I—but I didn't know why we did it.

Hives

The first day of second grade, my teacher, Mrs. Cooper, was getting acquainted with the forty or so members of her new class.
"Randall, do they call you Randy?" He would nod. And so it went:
James became Jimmy, Linda stayed Linda. But when she called
out "Margaret Pauley," I was too shy to speak up and say my
name was Janie, so I was Margaret Pauley for one whole year.

I loved Mrs. Cooper—if they manufactured second-grade
teachers, she would be the prototype—but in my entire school
career, the only time I was ever punished, it was by Mrs. Cooper,
and of all things, for talking! But I was innocent. She had picked
the wrong Margaret; it should have been Margaret Rush sitting
on the floor under the blackboard in the front of the room when
my mother unexpectedly walked in the door to visit. I believe
Mrs. Cooper was as embarrassed as I was, and she deftly swept
me up and sent me back to my desk before my mother noticed.
But twenty minutes later, my mother—and I, with one eye
swollen shut—were walking out the door again. That was my introduction to hives.

Maybe that was when my mother took me to that doctor
who said, "Janie is a nervous child, and she'll have to be careful

her whole life." I don't think he meant for Janie to hear it, much less remember it all these years later.

Second grade was the same year Daddy won a trip to Mexico in a sales contest, and my parents went to Acapulco for a week. Richard Warren's grandmother came to stay with Ann and me. That week, instead of Cheerios, I had toast with butter and lots of sugar for breakfast. I think it was also the last time the underside of the sofa faced the ceiling in the living room. A good time was had by all, in other words, and when Mom and Daddy came back, they had enough items for show-and-tell to last the rest of the year—maracas, mounted horns, a leather vest, silver trinkets! I couldn't say my name out loud, but I could stand in front of the room and shake my maracas! Show-*off*-and-tell was more like it. I could not wait for my turn.

In third grade I was cast in the coveted role of the princess in a scene from a story in our reader. It was such a thrilling prospect that I took extra care ironing my white blouse the night before—but not enough care. I touched the hot iron to my wrist, and it made an ugly, bubbly blister that was most obvious when I was standing in front of the room holding a third-grade reader. Still, I liked the attention.

Daddy was a man always in motion—even at rest in his ubiquitous rocking chair. He spent much of his life on the road, yet nothing made him happier on his one week of vacation a year than to get right back in the car and drive some more. He'd strap a folding rocker to the roof of the car, stay up late making an odd assortment of sandwiches (bologna and pickles and horseradish), pack the cooler with Pepsi, Fig Newtons, and Hershey bars. By four A.M., he was up again, and the loading continued in the darkened driveway. Loading the trunk meticulously was a 3–D puzzle. With Mom in her place and a Thermos of coffee between them, we would back out of the driveway, and a clock would start running in his head. Daddy, a traveling salesman, had the stamina of his trade, and, fortified by the coffee and an occasional power nap by the side of the road, he'd drive a thousand miles at a go; he could drive all night and for the same reason the truckers did—to "make good time." Always on a timetable. If he estimated our time of arrival at the Holiday Inn at two o'clock, we would expect to be unloading luggage at two–fifteen.

Daddy was not a car nut—he just loved to drive. He liked to cruise at seventy or seventy-five. If he used the horn, it was only a short tap. He'd never lean on it punitively. However, when driving, he was not the perfect gentleman that he was in every other respect. Behind the wheel he was aggressive. Confident. In control.

During those long drives in the company car there was nothing much to do—reading made me carsick. Watching Ann read or even thinking about Ann reading made me carsick. The only conversation over the whine of the road and the air whistling through open windows was "turn up the radio" or "change the station." Sometimes up and down the dial there was nothing but people shouting to Jesus. Driving through lonely mountains where there wasn't a house to be seen, you could understand why people thought they'd need to shout for God to hear.

To save time, of course, bathroom breaks were kept to the bare minimum and often conducted in tall grass. Being the littlest, I frequently found that the distance between my buns and the shorts at my ankles was insufficient. Once my damp little underpants were ingeniously tied to the radio antenna to dry, whipping in the wind as we sped through Ohio. A lot of people got to enjoy them, because Daddy was one of the great passing artists of his generation.

Another car on his side of the line was a challenge he couldn't ignore. He'd apply a little extra gas, pull left, press the pedal down, ease effortlessly back into our lane. Sometimes he'd shoot past a whole series of cars, and we'd be at the head of the line. I rode shotgun—on the lookout for trouble he might miss. Unlike Mom and Ann, who were often sound asleep, I had to be wide awake to watch out for Daddy.

Driving was full of contests. How far could he go after the gas gauge read *empty?* I knew when we were running low—I was generally watching over his shoulder. On one of our road trips, a two-lane stretch of Florida highway was taking us through the Everglades. We were plowing through a torrential downpour, and you could barely see the front of the car. I could see trucks barrel by us, and I knew trucks were behind us too. There was no shoulder on which to pull over at the side of the road—just swamp. We were out of gas, or would be any second, and nobody was sleeping now. Nobody was talking; we were focusing all our anxiety into the wish that a gas station would appear like an oasis in the rain before we rolled to a stop and were crushed from behind, or shoved into the jaws of an alligator. Somehow we made it. We always did. Whoever or whatever Daddy was dueling with had lost again. Every time Daddy filled 'er up to the max, he'd won.

"Making good time" meant pushing on for as long as there was light left in the day or gas in the tank, even as Ann and I whined every time we passed another sign that said MOTEL, SWIMMING POOL. Finally, we'd pull over, happy to swim in the dark somewhere in Alabama or Georgia. How my mother enjoyed these vacations was a mystery to me, until I grew up and understood the pleasure of doing nothing in a beautiful place.

And so the trip would go. Before dawn, Mom would rouse me from bed again, a bowl of Cheerios waiting and a hot plate going to refill the Thermos—instant coffee, which Daddy liked *hot hot*

hot. Whispering, we'd steal out to the car, wet with Southern dew, and plow on into the predawn light.

Many years later, when I was pregnant with twins and Daddy was at the wheel on a desolate stretch of highway along the Florida Panhandle coast, I was again focused on the needle that was pointing to *empty.* Though I threatened to name his first grandchildren Methyl and Ethyl if he passed by one more gas station, he would not stop. That time he was dueling with me. He won the battles. I usually won the wars.

Mom's lamp was the light we left on when we went out. It was the glow at the foot of the stairs that said "Mommy's here." When her lamp was on, I felt safe. Maybe she left the light on while she was in the hospital.

1963

I was coming along slowly. I had eventually gotten hair in abundance, as is often the case with babies born with little hair. When my permanent teeth came in a little "si–foddlin," my parents sent me to Dr. Rolenzo A. Hanes. Orthodontia for two daughters was not an insignificant portion of their annual income. This was a measure of my mother's hopes for her daughters' chances in life and the value my father placed upon attractiveness.

In seventh grade at Woodview Junior High School, when Mrs. Spilker measured me for the "crop tops" we would be making in her home–ec class, my "bust" strained the tape at twenty-five inches! "Why, you're one of the little ones!" she exclaimed behind the screen. I lived in dread that news of my little ones would be reported at the Spilkers' dinner table and Ricky Spilker would inform all our classmates at Woodview Junior High School. My fears were not completely unfounded, as later a friend told how she leapt to my defense when the topic of my flat chest came up. "I told them you just wore loose clothes," she solemnly assured me. In spite of my arrested development, I was actually doing okay. I wore a gold *W* on my chest. I thought I was a cheerleader for life.

• • •

One spring day in 1963, Mom had come downstairs crying. She told Ann she was bleeding heavily: She was frightened. By the time I got home, she had gone to the hospital in an ambulance.

Daddy started spending less time on the road and more time at the hospital than at home—he went back every evening after dinner. He had quite a poker face, because whatever story he fed us, we swallowed it whole. My cluelessness was rooted in his policy of not leaving clues. Daddy could never speak the word *cancer*. He used one of his unique euphemisms: "bad cells."

There were clues that Mommy was sicker than he let on. One of them was his new habit of using the phone in the basement. Another was the inexplicably mournful face the ladies at church wore when they asked how our mother was. "Fine, thank you," we said. I had no reason to believe otherwise. I didn't know what she had had until I was forty-five and I saw her medical records. It said: "ovarian carcinoma."

Kids weren't allowed in hospitals—I knew that because I'd had to wave at Ann from the parking lot when she had appendicitis. But one day the nuns let us break the rules: I read nothing into this highly unusual gesture, though they wouldn't let us stay long, because Mom had cobalt pellets inside her. I accepted the news that my mother was radioactive with the implicit confidence that doctors and nuns surely knew what they were doing. If the purpose of this special visit was for us to see each other for the last time, nobody let on.

I turned "lucky thirteen" on Halloween that year and can still remember all my presents—my first straight skirt, a coordinating vest, a medallion necklace like all the girls were wearing then, a red hobo-style purse with a lucky horseshoe, and a can of Dinty Moore beef stew. But I barely recall the year that my mother was ill. I don't remember being scared or even missing her.

. . .

My mother beat the odds and my parents began to plan for the future—they started to look at model homes in a nearby development. It wasn't far away, but definitely a step closer to the handsome Cleaver home on TV. The development was called Tempo. Set in shady lots on a street they called a lane were several furnished model homes, each with an attached garage, a foyer, a family room, a utility room, a kitchen with modern appliances, and up to five bedrooms. One of the bedrooms was decorated with a little girl in mind; it was pink—suffused with pink. I later found out that nothing but the lightbulb was actually pink.

My parents were enthralled, but they didn't lose their heads. They chose the Newport, the most modest of the model homes, but they picked a choice lot—it had sixteen trees. It strained my imagination to think we were going to be people who lived in an antique-brick ranch house. It strained my patience to wait for a house to be built, but it took no time at all! Ground was broken and a basement appeared, then plywood floors—Daddy and I liked to visit every evening after dinner. When the framing went up, I could sit in my "room"—my very first own room (not that I had yearned for one). There was a small problem: My bedroom had two windows, Ann's only one. Daddy was sensitive to the appearance of favoritism, so hers was embellished with a vanity and sink.

Our old house had a FOR SALE sign in the front yard. I wasn't paying attention to the implications when prospective buyers dropped in, and I didn't consider the meaning of leaving: that my childhood wouldn't be coming along, and I would never again run outside to play. My forsythia bush and my tree would grow on without me; the little chink in the hedge was probably gone already—the Falconburys had moved away.

And maybe childhood had already ended the night in 1964

when Daddy called me in to watch *The Ed Sullivan Show*—the Beatles! When Christmas 1964 came, we were settled in our new
house, and I learned the limits of my parents' prosperity. My "big"
present that year was from Grandma—a machine-made quilt in a
gold and white pattern to match my furniture. Consumed with
guilty feelings, I waited all day for someone to say, "Kidding!"

No more rooms got paneled or wallpapered. Daddy and I
didn't have projects together after we moved. His cherry mantel
over the fireplace represented a hundred hours or more of sanding,
staining, and polishing, but that was solitary labor. The patio was
designed in his head—the measuring and calculating. During the
digging and hauling, he kept a running tally of how many wheel-
barrows of soil he hauled away, how many bags of sand he
poured—savoring the opportunity to make a good story out of it.

The patio was his new headquarters of a summer evening—
in a rocker in perpetual motion, always with a soft drink at his
side, a newspaper in his lap, often with a flock of children twit-
tering about. Sometimes these children, whose names I didn't
know, would knock at the door asking, "Can Mr. Pauley come
out?" They were hoping to watch a squirrel take a peanut off his
shoe again, and to stay for a chat. Even the squirrels got to know
him, while I was squandering my chances.

He spent less time on the road, though each promotion
meant an upgrade of the company car in the garage. He stopped
hearing our prayers—we weren't little "kiddies" anymore. Now
he was the one listening for the crunch of gravel in the drive at
night and I was the one taking the waiting for granted.

I did join Daddy on the porch once in a while, and on a hot
summer evening I picked up the glass beside his rocking chair
and took a sip without asking. I expected a Coke, and it wasn't a
Coke. It was a curious thing, but I filed it away along with the incident with Uncle Henry and a swizzle stick I found in his suitcase, and a couple of other things I'd made note of when I was
only five and we lived at the old house.

Somebody had noticed that our cat, Lucky, was bleeding and saw her climb up the trunk of Daddy's car (which was always covered with paw prints). Of course, we all had to investigate and followed her to the attic of the garage, where we discovered three mewing newborn kittens in a nail keg left over from when Daddy had built the garage.

It's hard to imagine anything taking my attention away from kittens, but I did notice a box with ornate bottles containing golden and amber liquids. How a kid knows what a liquor bottle is I do not know, but I knew that's what they were. I asked Daddy about them, and why they weren't full. "Evaporation" is what he told me.

Another time when I was small I asked if he ever drank beer. He said, "Maybe on a hot day."

As a morose freshman home from college, I confided to my mother: "I wish I was back in high school and happy again."

I was dumbfounded by her reply: "I never knew you to be happy."

High school might not be the best place to look for happy people. But in the 1968 *Warren Wigwam*, you could find Janie Pauley's smiling face in any number of enviable poses—speech and debate, DAR Good Citizen, Fall Homecoming (court), and Winter Homecoming (court). In high school, I occupied an uncommon number of pedestals. How did my mother miss all that happiness?

1965

My fourteen-year-old identity at Warren Central High School was obliterated in the fall of my sophomore year by a gift that came out of the blue. It was disguised as a crushing disappointment.

In September of tenth grade, I tried out for junior varsity cheerleader in the gym. Shrieks of teenage jubilation reverberated around the cinder-block walls when the names of those chosen were called—but not mine. Names went cartwheeling down the halls, my name following along in a whisper, summoning the one person who was listening for it—my sister. I dissolved into her arms: such a scene. It was the saddest day of my life—and the luckiest.

It was my introduction into the vast varsity sisterhood of dashed dreams. Since sixth grade, I had worn the coveted sweater emblazoned with a large letter. The white pleated skirt, the tennis shoes that practically glowed after every coat of white liquid shoe polish—they were mine. Though I couldn't do flips or splits, or even jump very high, I had made no other plan.

They say that when one door closes, another one opens. The problem is, the first one doesn't close; it slams shut in your tear-streaked face, while the other one opens so uneventfully you don't know you've passed through a golden door. That's how it was with me in 1965, and so often since. Life comes out of the blue.

Sadder but wiser is the girl who knows that "try, try again" means try something different. Lucky is the girl who has no choice. It was late on a Saturday near the end of September. My sister, then a senior, and Judy, my new best friend, were chattering excitedly about their first day at a speech tournament. They "bombed out," in the vernacular of the initiated, meaning they spent the day drinking Cokes with hundreds of other kids. But they still rode home like champions; Warren Central High School was a speech and debate powerhouse.

Suddenly, all my Fridays and Saturdays for the rest of my young life were wide open, so, with Judy, I signed up for a novice debate tournament. What we lacked in preparation and experience we made up for—somehow. We were undefeated when we decided to retire with a perfect record: four for four. We'd begun to notice that the other novice debaters, mostly small, intense boys, were arriving with large file boxes stuffed with index cards filled with facts and figures. Judy and I had boxes, too, but they were about the size of ones you'd fill with recipes. We noticed the kids who competed in "extemp"—extemporaneous speaking— were carrying only newsmagazines. The idea of speaking extemporaneously—which is to say without having to prepare—also appealed to our work ethic.

So every Saturday in schools around Indianapolis and central Indiana, we picked up slips of paper with topics drawn from the indexes of *Time, Newsweek,* and *U.S. News & World Report:* RED CHINA: PAPER TIGER? (no); JOHN LINDSAY: IS HE PRESIDENTIAL TIMBER? (yes). Thirty minutes to compose a seven-minute speech and persuade a judge that you'd been weighing the balance of payments for years! (A perfect rehearsal for all those seven-minute interviews on *Today*, also drawn from the day's headlines.)

Judy and I were no longer a team, as extemp is a solo event. We were competitors. Our very first outing, a large novice tournament at Ball State University in Muncie, was the only time we would ever compete with boys and girls together. Judy finished second, and I finished first. Picking up a trophy in an auditorium with hundreds of teenagers was pretty thrilling. We were hooked.

After throwing up in the cafeteria in first grade and being falsely accused of talking in second grade, the only other trouble came in tenth grade—and it involved another favorite teacher, Mrs. Effman. She was younger than the average teacher, prettier and really smart. That's why it was destabilizing that she was so put out with me when I turned in an essay written in pencil, not pen, and she said so publicly in a rather sharp tone. When you get in trouble on average only once a decade—and completely out of the blue—it is a shattering experience beyond all proportion. I spent the rest of the period trying not to cry.

Sometime that year, she also nominated me for a national English-student award that a boy in Ann's grade actually won. I was an odd candidate, insofar as I was demonstrably not the best English student in our classroom or even in my row. At the time, I interpreted it as the gesture of a very good teacher trying to build some self-esteem in a girl who might have been a better student than she knew.

In the sixties, daddies who encouraged their precocious daughters were playing with fire: female ambition. Ann got a twelve-foot-long telescope for Christmas one year and a chemistry set another. But when she expressed interest in becoming a doctor, the minister from our church was invited to the house to counsel her that marriage and family and the medical profession didn't go together. And she shouldn't think about dating Catholic boys, either. I never got such a meeting. When I reached dating age, my parents were just relieved to see a boy at the door.

1967

The summer after my junior year of high school, my parents drove me to Indiana University in Bloomington for Girls' State. Delegates selected from every high school in the state were moving into college dormitory rooms. Girls' State was a mock-government program sponsored by the American Legion Auxiliary. Everybody had to run for something, but it was not in my nature to shoot for the top. This was the effect our coach Harry Wilfong had on his kids: I could do it for him or not; it was up to me.

The afternoon I won my party's nomination for governor was more thrilling than being elected Governor Janie Pauley, or just about anything else I've ever experienced. We were organized into four counties. I made my little speech, and so did the others. When the voting began, I was sitting with my county on the far left of the auditorium. The balloting started inconclusively—a smattering for one candidate or another—through the first and second ballots. But then, at the end of the third ballot, the county on the opposite side of the auditorium—hundreds of girls I didn't know—cast every vote for me! After my election as governor, I went on to veto most of the bills the legislature sent up for my signature.

As a delegate to Girls Nation later that summer of 1967, our own President Johnson (Cathy) appointed me secretary of state and my real-life counterpart, Dean Rusk, showed me the red telephone and said, "I hope it never rings."

• • •

In the fall of 1967 I was making an appearance before a local chapter of the American Legion as governor of Girls' State. Mom drove me there in her Dodge Dart, and together we were seated in the front row of a hall packed with people sitting on folding chairs on either side of a long center aisle. When the honor guard strode up bearing banners and the American flag, all rose, including the leaders of the legionnaires, standing on the dais in full legion regalia. They snapped to attention, hurling crisp military salutes to the flag—and likewise did my mother! To my stunned surprise as I laid my own hand across my heart, my mother's right arm whipped through the air in a fantastic salute.

Instantly, she regained control of her senses and tried to withdraw her pose, thankful that she hadn't yelled "Attennnn*hut*!!!" Being considerate, scores of people who surely saw it pretended not to. But poor Mom didn't have the cover of long hair, as I did, to hide her heaving shoulders when spasms of giggles welled up at random moments for the remainder of the afternoon. There was never a time during the rest of her life, even after all her strokes, that I couldn't make her laugh with a salute.

We shared the laughter so easily, but not the pain.

From the age of four, God had provided me with best friends; Donna, Carol, and then Judy were all girls next door. My freshman year in college at Indiana University was a test of skills I'd never had to learn—how to make friends. I did not ace that test.

First semester in the dorm, my roommate was an upperclassman with an established group of friends. I was a friendly girl but very shy. Once, a guy I knew dropped by unexpectedly and found me eating alone; I nearly broke my own heart with the tale I fabricated about my friends eating earlier.

The next semester I moved to a different floor and suddenly had friends galore. Someone in the dorm was charting dating trends, and on our floor I ranked number one in quantity and last in quality. After freshman year, my social life tapered off, until most of the guys I saw on Saturday nights were delivering tacos. But I never had to watch *The Mary Tyler Moore Show* alone. I pledged a sorority, Kappa Kappa Gamma, and God provided seventy "sisters next door"—including my old friend Judy, who transferred to IU sophomore year.

Spring semester that year, a friend and I were doing some math, calculating how we could graduate a semester early, inaugurating a lifetime pattern: I know when it's time to leave, even when I don't know where I'm going.

I didn't have a lot of disposable income in college after buying cigarettes and pizza, but I bought a copy of a Doors' album at the record store next to the "People's Park" on Kirkwood Avenue. I didn't own a stereo. My motives are mysterious, which probably was the point of it—a private statement about the singularity, the poetry, and especially "the mystery" of me. I walked the leafy pathways of Bloomington in my jeans–and–work–shirt combo, waiting for love to happen out of the blue. I encountered a flasher once, but I left IU without ever having fallen in love.

A university spokesman later said I "hadn't made much of a splash" in Bloomington. My Class of '72 classmate Mark Spitz (seven Olympic gold medals) had set the bar awfully high.

Getting on the wrong bus that first day of first grade may have been a metaphor. It told me that the delightful little girl can get lost when she's alone in the world. A little malingerer sitting alone at the top of the stairs in Dr. Denton's, feeling guilty about staying home from school (the oldest trick in the book, a tummy ache) is the same girl who lived with her sister for three days after Christmas break rather than face her bleak life in the college freshman dorm. She's the same girl whose office at NBC in New York was "devoid of personality." And she's the same girl whose picture was on the cover of national magazines in 1976.

The girl whose timbers could be shivered for a reprimand over the use of a pencil instead of a pen and who broke out in hives when she was sent to the front of the classroom. The same girl who was too shy to say her name but who couldn't wait to shake her maracas in front of the class for show-and-tell—and her pom-poms in the gym.

Later, the same girl whose blood pressure went *down* on live TV would have palpitations at home in her apartment alone.

PART V

Jane

According to the Things Falling out of Heaven Theory, which I first conceived of in high school, the most likely moment for something incredible to happen to me was the moment when I was most certain that nothing ever would.

"Nothing comes from nothing, nothing ever could." In this refrain from *The Sound of Music*, Maria concludes that she "must have done something good." Bless her heart, she can conceive of no other explanation for the happy turn her life has taken than that she must have done something to deserve it. When wonderful things happened to me, I did not arrive at the same conclusion. As a teenager, I had already noticed how often special things came my way—and in a cyclical pattern I described as the Things Falling out of Heaven Theory. This theory predicted that something incredible—and unexpected—would happen only after I had reached the certain conclusion that my string of good luck had ended forever. At this bleak moment: boom! An opportunity, a phone call, an introduction would change my life.

This lucky pattern not only continued but accelerated in my early adult life. A life so conspicuously charmed demanded an explanation—certainly one better than "I must have done something good." But I was aware of no satisfactory explanation.

It had not been my dream to have a career in broadcast journalism, it was just my best idea. Taking the sensible advice of my freshman counselor in college, I didn't major in radio and TV, but I told my roommates weeks before graduation that I'd stay in

Indianapolis if I got a job at a TV station, as if jobs like that just came out of the blue. My prospects looked pretty grim.

On the eve of my graduation it dawned on me that I still didn't know what I was going to do with my life! I called home in tears at four A.M. and my father pulled up at six A.M. to take me home for a few days. I guess I had kept my feelings to myself most of the time, because my mother talked about that call for the rest of her life. Always a little younger than my classmates, and a little ahead of myself, I had plotted an early graduation, as if I was in a hurry to get somewhere—but where? I called it "the black hole that is my future." In the early seventies, "entry level" still meant a mandatory typing test for a woman. I was once put before an electric typewriter and blazed my way to eleven words a minute. My father suggested I look into a career as a receptionist—like the attractive young women he knew from sales calls.

He had had doubts about his investment in my political science degree and, in a fateful gesture, had buttonholed a fellow attendee at a downtown Presbyterian Men's meeting, asking, "What's Janie going to do with a degree in poli sci?" The fact that Gordon St. Angelo was a Presbyterian compensated for the fact that he was not a Republican—like both of my parents. He was the chairman of the Indiana Democratic State Central Committee. Thanks to Daddy, I got a summer job working for the Democrats: fifty dollars a week. Though my mother was never reconciled to this favor—or the fact that I borrowed her car to work there—it was the right time and the right place.

After graduation I was back at Indiana Democratic headquarters, at twice the salary (one hundred dollars a week) and with a title—administrative assistant. Most days, I filled up wastebaskets with mistyped envelopes and letters. Before that, fear of the future had overcome fear of the phone, and I had done something entirely out of character. Sitting on the edge of my canopy bed at home, I picked up my low-mileage Princess phone and called

WISH–TV anchorman Mike Ahern. Making a speech was easy, but a phone call was so very hard! I would have to say, "Mr. Ahern, you may not remember me, but…." What if he didn't?

We had met four years before, when I was a senior in high school and, as governor of Girls's State, was named youth chairman of the tuberculosis fund; Mike was the chairman. He remembered, and invited me to come by the station. I was calling for career advice, but I imagined being shown my office before I left that day. Instead, I got an invitation to dinner. Mike included Channel Eight statehouse reporter Frank Phillipi. That was significant, because Frank would later play a key role in launching my TV career.

At Democratic headquarters, I had gotten acquainted with many local reporters—print, radio, TV. I was the long–haired girl at State Committee, but Frank was the only reporter who knew that I would want to know it if Channel Eight was hiring. They were looking for "a female–type person" is how he phrased it. I qualified. Though that was my only qualification, I called news director Lee Giles with no hesitation; I was very confident. Although I didn't know it, Lee had never agreed to interview anyone without experience or a journalism degree. He preferred both. I had neither.

After an interview, he asked me to write up a sample newscast. I was at least a fair writer, and with my high school extemporaneous–speaking experience, I was conversant with current events and knew how to organize ideas. Typing was my biggest problem; and script paper came in quadruplicate pages. I was shown the studio, the first I'd ever seen and, sitting in Mike's place at the Big News desk, read my pages without a teleprompter, just looking down and up again into the camera. I felt so completely comfortable, I caught my mind wandering! That was scary. But at the end, the young cameraman volunteered that I was the best.

The general manager, Robert McConnell, was a leading Republican fund-raiser. He had the final say. I wore my best, and possibly my only, dress, a demure Albert Nipon navy polka dot with empire waist and white cuffs and collar. I made my hair as inconspicuous as possible, in a ponytail pulled straight off my face. Noting the opposition party on my résumé, McConnell asked me if I could be an unbiased reporter, and I answered truthfully: "Yes."

I was Indianapolis's newest TV reporter (temporary, probationary for ninety days) two weeks before Election Day 1972. I was looking forward to my first election-night coverage, and all eyes were on Walter Cronkite at seven o'clock, when *CBS Evening News* went on the air. The very first thing he said was, "The polls in Indiana are closed...." And that was about it for the night. Nineteen seventy-two was a good year to be a Republican in Indiana and a bad year to be a reporter.

I got my first apartment. It was time to take an even bigger step. I hadn't had a haircut since at least 1966. But when Indianapolis's premier stylist saw me sitting under two and a half feet of hair, he said, "I'm not cutting that." I don't know why, exactly — whether he feared legal action or emotional repercussions — but I left with my hair intact. No rushing this growing up; I should wait to get a new identity before I lopped off the old one.

1975

After three years in Indianapolis, I was a senior member of the reporting staff, a veteran of twenty-one months as a noon and weekend anchor, and ambitious for a promotion. Mike Ahern had been without a co-anchor on the weekday edition of the six o'clock news. I was filling in as a temporary, interim co-anchor, but station owners in New York decided Indianapolis was "not ready for a female news anchor." I was disappointed, but it was conventional wisdom among a generation of news executives that audiences didn't want to hear the news in a woman's voice.

A smattering of long–distance phone calls suggested the wisdom was becoming less conventional. Without my knowledge, I had been included on a videotape being circulated among stations by one of the newly proliferating news consultants, so-called news doctors. Apparently, the entire newsroom was wise to these phone calls from Buffalo or Grand Rapids. I passed on the opportunity to take on a Philadelphia phenomenon named Jessica Savitch. Her name alone was intimidating. But when WSB in Atlanta sent a plane ticket, I was excited to go, though it felt like cheating. Everything seemed to go really well—an audition as well as several interviews so low–key I wasn't sure they were interviews. But at the end of the day, station lawyers said that my so–called letter of agreement with WISH was as ironclad a contract as they'd ever seen. Since they were Southern gentlemen, I assumed I was being let down—gently.

The odds that a weekend anchor would be spotted rose considerably on a Memorial Day weekend, when half a million visitors were in Indianapolis for the Indy 500. The odds further favored a weekend anchor at WISH-TV, the CBS affiliate in Indianapolis in 1975. Thanks to the tsunami that CBS delivered every Saturday night following a lineup that included *M*A*S*H, All in the Family, The Bob Newhart Show, The Mary Tyler Moore Show,* and *The Carol Burnett Show,* my show was the most-watched local news show in the state. Unless there was breaking news, I could finish the lineup early and watch *The Mary Tyler Moore Show* myself—Mary Richards, not Barbara Walters, was the most famous newswoman in the country. But that particular Saturday I was more attentive. In the back of my mind, I thought, if anyone in town was watching the news at all that night, chances are they were watching Channel Eight. My intuition was right.

In early June, a man on the phone said, "I'm sorry, Miss

Pauley, but I don't know your first name." He identified himself as Ed Planer, from WMAQ-TV in Chicago. Chicago was the third-largest television market in the country, and WMAQ was owned and operated by NBC News. Mr. Planer wanted to see my reel, taking it for granted that I had one. A reel is a compilation of your greatest hits—basically, the work that shows a reporter or anchor to her best advantage. It was the odd TV reporter who didn't have a reel ready-made, in case opportunity came knocking, but I was the odd reporter who didn't. I had to scramble to figure out how people made a reel right under the noses of the employers they were conniving to leave.

I sent my reel up to Mr. Planer in Chicago, along with a short letter alerting him to the letter of agreement—with an addendum that I'd recently won an award for feature reporting. I wanted him to know about the award, but hoped he didn't ask to see the spot I won it for, because the audio track was entirely music, Gershwin's *An American in Paris*. With all the honking and beeping, I thought it would be great with quick-cut shots of cars sliding and getting stuck in snow. I stayed warm in the car while the reporter got the shots, and I probably sipped a Coke while he edited the film. My reel was heavy on features, with better-than-average writing; perhaps it showed that my camera skills were a lot better than average, but I was not likely to be hired on the strength of my reporting.

Right away, Mr. Planer called again, inviting me to fly up to Chicago after work to audition after the ten o'clock news on a Wednesday early in June. I felt like I was cheating again. I caught a plane to Chicago—possibly my first visit since an eighth-grade field trip to the famous Field Museum of Natural History, which I remember chiefly because it had been a good hair day. After his ten o'clock newscast, I took a seat in the studio beside the venerable Floyd Kalber. I read a few pages. I'd never used a teleprompter before. It's like riding a bike: At first, you fall down a lot.

Otherwise, reading the news was not a problem and the camera was not intimidating. Floyd could have made short work of me, but when we ad-libbed some cross talk, he pitched me questions about Indiana politics, something I knew about. It felt good. When executive producer Paul Beaver walked me out, he asked, "How old did you say you were?" in a tone that seemed to say, "You couldn't possibly be twenty-four."

I flew home and went to work as if nothing had happened. After a while, hearing nothing from Chicago, I wondered if nothing *had* happened. Then Ed Planer came in person to Indianapolis "with a bag full of money," as he later liked to tell the story. Only after he made me a breathtaking offer did he think to ask what I was currently making. Realizing he had given me a raise of almost 400 percent, he made me promise never to tell anyone—so you'll have to do the math. The salary Ed Planer offered me was staggering—$55,000.

The mystery is how such a "nervous child" became so comfortable in a field that according to studies, scares most people more than death—public speaking.

After I got the news about the offer from WMAQ in Chicago, I jumped out of my 1972 Opel and burst into the house, excited to tell my father. Maybe it was the kind of news that is typically preceded by "You'd better sit down." Daddy wasn't prepared for my good news, and I wasn't prepared for the look on his face. Whatever it was, it wasn't joy. The figure I named was more than twice what he had paid for our house.

That night at dinner, my father and my boyfriend, an Indianapolis newspaper reporter, did not seem much in the mood for celebrating. My father was irritable and annoyed. The stated reason was that he liked bread with his dinner and the restaurant I had picked didn't serve bread.

I could not fathom what the matter was; he was so sweet and famously even-tempered. I hardly knew he could have a bad mood! He never swore, except to say "Fire!" or "For the gee whiz!" when he was seriously provoked, which wasn't often. He spanked me only once (he called spanking "paddling," which softened the blow only a little). The look of disappointment on his face was bigger punishment by far.

His behavior at that dinner seemed so odd. I could not explain it, except to conclude that I'd done something that had disappointed Daddy.

There was a commercial on TV for a while that featured armored trucks full of pennies dropping from the sky upon unsuspecting pedestrians. It struck me as a perfect metaphor for a mixed blessing—pennies from heaven, and getting hit by a truck. I wonder if that's how my father felt when my career came barreling out of the blue.

June 1975

In the spring of 1975, things were falling from heaven right and left, with periods of dejection in between. As it turned out, my one-page letter of agreement with WISH-TV really was pretty ironclad, and the same station owners who had thought Indianapolis was not ready for me were now not ready to let me go. I was unaccustomed to having men fight over me. After hard negotiating, the final agreement was that I would be released from my contract—but not until Channel Eight found my replacement.

In the meantime, WMAQ was free to announce our happy news. The Chicago press had previously reported that a talent search was under way at Channel Five for a co-anchor. This was newsworthy because anchorman Floyd Kalber, who was practically a Chicago icon, had always worked solo, while the other network affiliates had gone successfully to anchor teams—all men. So when Kalber's putative co-anchor turned out to be a woman, that was bigger news. And when that woman was half Floyd's age—the same age as his daughter, in fact—it was practically a scandal. I had no idea what I was in for.

Biding my time, in Indianapolis, I started reading Chicago newspapers. One day I saw my postage-stamp-size picture on the cover of the *Chicago Tribune*! Right there at the newsstand I flipped to the story inside. It was a TV column in which an "unnamed staffer" is quoted as saying I had "the IQ of a cantaloupe." The only WMAQ staffers who knew me had hired me and weren't likely to be whispering to TV critics. I felt suckerpunched. They kept coming: Another critic called me a "hood ornament." Every paper in town took a shot. It didn't take an investigative reporter to get the goods on me; it was all there on my driver's license: hair color, blond; eye color, blue; age, twentyfour; residency—*not* Illinois. Meanwhile, WISH-TV took so long finding my replacement that NBC threatened to withdraw the offer. It was two months before I actually arrived in Chicago. By then, my welcoming committee had worn itself out, and I slipped into town thinking the worst was behind me.

Chicago is a city that never fails to surpass my memory of how beautiful—even glamorous—it is. I thought finding a place to live would be fun, until I asked a parking lot attendant for directions. He recognized my face. "Are you that new girl at Channel Five?" he asked. I beamed.

He said, "Poor baby."

I did what any scared animal would do: I raced to the tallest tree.

Chicago is famously a city of neighborhoods, but I opted for a towering glass apartment building just off Michigan Avenue, the perfect choice for an out-of-town transient. The lake was to the east, but my apartment faced west—the less expensive side. It had a killer view. From the fifty-fourth floor it looked at the flight path into O'Hare. I could see the sleek silhouettes of planes coming and going in ones and twos, night and day, ten miles away. In between, the expressways pulsed with cars and trucks—white lights streaming in, red lights out. Against the wind off the lake, the building creaked and groaned. The clothes in my closet swung back and forth. When you walked in my front door, the afternoon light smacked you in the face. It was not the best choice for a lonely girl who needed to build a life from scratch.

Personal style or taste hadn't occurred to me yet. My decorating inspirations came from TV. I liked the bookcases on *The Bob Newhart Show*, but they were too expensive. My salary sounded substantial, but it wasn't money in the bank. So my Sony TV stayed balanced on the same boards and bricks I'd had in college. It all looked conspicuously barren to me: I was the stereotypical single girl with cats. This may be the norm at twenty-four, but being the object of media attention makes one look at life even more self-consciously.

I felt more at home at work. I ate meals there. I had friends there, though working the late shift meant they went home without me, commuting as far as Indiana and the Wisconsin border. My old friends were scattered around the country, in new jobs or new marriages. But when my sister came to town, there was no shortage of things to do after we made chocolate chip pancakes for breakfast. The corner store was Bonwit's, I. Magnin, or Marshall Field's. Michigan Avenue was a revelation to the Pauley sisters. We were literally bowled over one Saturday morning. First Ann stumbled and then I went tumbling after—both of us splayed on one of the most glamorous sidewalks in America.

Floyd had a party at one of Chicago's finest restaurants and encouraged me to bring a date. I took my boyfriend, Bill Shaw, from Indianapolis. Bill dressed with a certain flair; he owned many pairs of Frye boots, which he cared for with loving attention. He was a detail man—he ironed his T-shirts and his blue jeans. The boots, jeans, T-shirts, and a cowboy-style shirt made up a uniform that, like a Rorschach test, would ferret out snobs and phonies. So it was with some trepidation that I invited Bill to join us—not knowing how he'd finesse the dress requirements, which called for jacket and tie. He compromised, arriving in a denim suit and his best Frye boots.

Before long, I became aware of activity under Bill's side of the table and realized he'd decided to make himself more comfortable by removing his boots! I interpreted this to be a test of how phony I had become since I got my fancy job in Chicago. I had not become an urban sophisticate overnight, but I took for granted that at a four-star restaurant, or even a diner, patrons keep their shoes on. This is what made the escapade such a delight for him, I'm sure. But Floyd must have had the same gene, because before the night was out, he had taught all of us at the table how to hang spoons from the tips of our noses. He was such a master, he had them dangling simultaneously from his nose, his chin, and both cheeks.

Having an out-of-town boyfriend was a mixed blessing; it meant I had a life, but it wasn't in Chicago. A relationship that is a tale of two cities is not likely to have a happy ending.

One of my first assignments in television as a reporter at WISH–TV had been a feature about a palm reader. The first thing she did, of course, was turn over my hand. After she studied my palm, she observed, "You don't do much housework." Then, looking up, she told me, "You have a lot of ambition but not a lot of drive." I stayed puzzled by that paradox when, year after year, my presence on network television begged the question: Without drive, how did I get here?

1975–1976

The midsummer barrage of withering publicity arguably did me a favor by setting the bar low, where I like it. To exceed expectations, I merely had to look smarter than a cantaloupe. I also had the kind of name recognition it could take years to establish, the poor–baby sympathy factor, and a considerable number of my enemies' enemies—which amounted to some very powerful friends. *Sun-Times* columnist Ron Powers, for instance, had a Pulitzer Prize, and he wrote of me, "Jane Pauley, ridiculed in advance of her WMAQ television news debut for being young, a woman, beautiful, and (gasp) a non–Chicagoan, made all the criticism seem a bit silly Monday night."

My morning–after reviews were fabulous. In the Tower Ticker column of the *Chicago Tribune*, I was judged to have "...confidence, competence, believability and warmth," and was given a 9½ rating on a 10–point scale. According to Irv Kupcinet, the influential gossip columnist of the *Chicago Sun-Times*: "Consensus in TV Circles: Channel 5 Came Up with a Winner." The head of a competing TV station predicted, "She's going to be around a long time." And a top executive of an independent TV station said, "I think they've got a winner."

Women all over town were watching the debut of Chicago's first woman anchor on a major evening show with trepidation; if I looked good, they looked good, and if I failed, it would reflect on them. The newswomen at Channel Two, the CBS affiliate, reportedly convened in the ladies' room after my first show. Their verdict: "Wasn't it great?"

Going from "hood ornament" to "Hoosier hotshot" was very gratifying and a relief, but I had lost something in the bargain. My life was now in the public domain. In Indianapolis, my comings and goings were never mentioned in the papers. I was playing in a different league now, and cultivating a public profile was part of the job. Some would regard being seen about town and getting my name in the columns as the best part of the job, but it was the part I was least prepared for. The wrong answer to the question "Whose dress is that?" I understood belatedly, is "Mine."

It was ironic that I discussed this turn in my life in an interview with a columnist from home: "There are pressures I never felt before back home in Indianapolis—pressures to dress a certain way, act a certain way, pressures to be seen certain places. People are recognizing me on the street—I'm being treated like a princess—and I have to keep my head. I don't want to lose control of my private life. It would be so easy for me to become a star and stop being Jane Pauley... but all I want to do is be myself.... I know it sounds trite, but that's the only person I know how to be."

I drew a line around my private life—such as it was—and posted a KEEP OUT sign at my door. Not even for a cover story in the *Chicago Tribune Sunday Magazine* would I relent and permit the requisite shot of "Jane at home." A visit to a flea market was a substitute photo op. The reporter, Marilyn Preston, thought it remarkable that someone so young had such a clear sense of personal boundaries. Though frustrated by me, Marilyn says she interpreted it as a sign of strength. It was also a sign of ambivalence about the all-consuming nature of my job. I have never called it a career.

Wondering about the distinction, I looked it up. The dictionary definition of *careerism* connotes a devotion to career at the expense of a personal life. Even though my personal life barely had a pulse, I hadn't intended to give it up and I wouldn't give it up. My life's work was going to have to work with my life—not the other way around.

Marilyn's story was titled "That Pauley Kid." It was long, insightful, and accurate—Marilyn counted every cigarette. My family was coming for Christmas the weekend the article came out. I called my sister in a panic: "You have to tell them!" I could smoke nine cigarettes in front of the *Chicago Tribune*, but my mother and father were not to know (officially)!

Even while ferociously protecting my privacy, I seemed practically eager to point out my shortcomings (and still do). For example, I drew Marilyn's attention to my "raggedy fingernails" and even volunteered, "The most interesting thing about me is my job." I'm candid almost to a fault: "I guess I really am two different people," I told Marilyn, verging on a genuine insight. "There's the Jane Pauley on the air and then there's me, and I'm not sure I understand the contradiction; but I'm not going to let it bother me."

That sounded like Janie talking.

A reader wrote a letter to the editor referring to "that Pauley Kid." On the screen, he said, I came across as a "cold, disgustingly arrogant, and condescending newscaster." Even my humor seemed "phony." But the Preston article had given him pause. "Just who is the real Jane Pauley?" he wondered.

I was a success on one level, and that was figuring out the difference between growing and changing, and what I just couldn't change.

"Barbara Walters said to tell you you're doing a good job." *Sun-Times* columnist Ron Powers was the messenger. Another person had already told me the same thing in exactly the same words. Why was I on Barbara's radar? It seemed significant, but what did it signify? Then an invitation arrived to fill in for Barbara when *Today* came to Chicago. I remembered Ed Planer's prediction, "On *Today* in three years!" I had been in Chicago fewer than three months. The evening before, I had met the handsome and low-key co-host Jim Hartz and the highbrow executive producer Stuart Schulberg (*Today* wasn't a "show," it was a "program"). I went to bed with a migraine, which was a blessing in disguise, because there is no better feeling than waking up without one.

Every Friday during the run-up to the bicentennial year, *Today* was visiting a different state. Barbara was traveling with President Ford in China. The state visit was doubly auspicious for me. It not only coincided with *Today*'s "Salute to Illinois," it was when NBC's White House reporter, Tom Brokaw, met and made a new friend in cartoonist Garry Trudeau—they tossed a Frisbee on the Great Wall.

A reporter dialed my parents' listed phone number looking for a comment on my first appearance on a network show. "Fairly good," was my mother's cautious reply, and then she added, "Janie always says her father is her worst critic."

I tried to shield my parents from the press. I don't know whether I was protecting them or myself. I didn't think we were strange—just very, very normal. No story there! But Daddy came to Chicago on business once and took me and a new friend of mine to dinner. He was irritable again. I was a little embarrassed when he was not his usual gracious self with the waiter. When he walked us home, he asked if the friend needed help with her "impedimenta," which I associated with the Roman legions. I hadn't heard the word since tenth-grade Latin. He wasn't acting normal. I was worried about him.

Newscenter Five in Chicago represented a complete newscast makeover—set graphics, new girl from Indianapolis—the works. Our set looked like a spaceship. It was meant to telegraph electronic journalism—our new Minicams and satellite trucks and reporters were "live on the scene" somewhere, every night. To emphasize the point, our digital theme music was accompanied by an oscillating red line at the bottom of the screen. I thought it conveyed an ambiguous message—perhaps a patient on life support. But the changes shot new life into the ratings, at least at first. By mid-January, however, columnist Gary ("IQ of a cantaloupe") Deeb was happy to report that Channel Five's ten o'-clock newscast was falling out of the pack. By April, on some nights, our show came in fifth in the ratings! A hometown paper reported, "Friends of Jane Pauley here are concerned that she may be the sacrificial lamb in that calamity known as WMAQ-TV, Chicago." According to insiders, I was "not in danger," but everyone else was.

Between newscasts one night, Floyd was going to dinner with an old friend, an NBC News executive from New York named

Joe Bartelme. Perhaps they were talking about Floyd's future, or mine. They urged me to come along, and though I'd already eaten, the waiter encouraged me to order a little something. He was wearing a tuxedo, so I obeyed. While Floyd and Joe waited, I scanned the menu for something I recognized and announced my decision, which met with the waiter's approval. Meanwhile, Joe told a funny story about a talent scout who went to some town and signed the wrong person, so naturally I wondered if Ed Planer had made a mistake. The waiter arrived with our selections, setting a little something in front of me—could these raw clams be the "cherrystones" I had ordered?

I put one in my mouth, but it fought all the way down. I knew it would be very dicey to try another. But when the waiter came back, seeing only one missing, he looked troubled and hurt, so I explained, "Sometimes they don't agree with me," sounding worldly and self-assured, or so I thought.

By the time the Indy 500 came around again in May, Floyd Kalber had been airlifted to New York and was the new news anchor on *Today*. I had been demoted—taken off the ten o'clock news and paired at five with a new anchorman from Miami. Liberated from the strain of months-long uncertainty, I was more comfortable than I'd ever been in Chicago. But TV critics reported rumors that I wouldn't be around town much longer, and I believed them. We were all right.

I was unpacking my bag in a New York hotel when the phone rang. It was my sister calling with breaking news. She had read in her local paper that I was a finalist to replace Barbara Walters on *Today*.

I hadn't seen it coming, because the invitation to "fill in for Betty Furness" had omitted any reference to a tryout. That summer, America was treated to an unusual TV spectacle as NBC made finding a replacement for Barbara Walters on *Today* a summer reality show. The *Tribune* reported there had been "2000 applicants, boiled down to one hundred hopefuls." According to *Time*, NBC News executives screened 150 tapes of local and network newswomen, of whom four were invited to audition. Linda Ellerbee was NBC correspondent at the House of Representatives, Catherine (Cassie) Mackin was at the Senate and was more famously NBC's first female convention floor reporter, Kelly Lange was a local anchor in Los Angeles, and Betty Rollin was a veteran of both television and magazines. I was four years'out of college.

Ann's news kept me up for most of the night, and I fell asleep about forty-five minutes before my wake-up call. But when the red light on the camera went on, as I unself-consciously told a reporter later, "I immediately felt right at home." That's how young I was, but the red-light reflex was probably my competitive edge. I matched or beat all of them in experience before a live camera. Television hadn't started actively looking for newswomen to put on camera until the early seventies. Some talk about the Class of '72, referring to women who got their jobs, give or take, that year. I coined the phrase, having literally been a member of the Class of '72. My partner that morning was Lloyd Dobbins, who was filling in for Jim Hartz. Lloyd had an attitude that strongly conveyed "it didn't matter," which lowered the tension considerably. I had fun.

I advanced to the next level—a weeklong chemistry test with Tom Brokaw the second week of September. "Viewer mail is running in her favor, and she even speaks like Barbara Walters," it was reported. Cassie was also invited back—I watched her tryout from Chicago, most memorably the tough interview with the new Miss America that she shared with Tom, both of them fresh off the Watergate beat. Betty Furness was also belatedly acknowledged as a contender, having been rudely overlooked in the first round, for the obvious but unstated reason that she was too old: sixty.

Back in Chicago, where a pulse could be detected in the cadaver that was my career, I had another lunch with reporter Marilyn Preston of the *Tribune*, who had the distinction of being the only print reporter in town who, the year before, didn't react to my arrival "as if Typhoid Mary had signed on as Water Commissioner." Though her story makes clear how I savor the prospect of getting the job, I sound rather like the lucky winner of a contest to see which virgin gets to be thrown into the volcano: "Imagine being twenty-five and single and going to *the* city of the world with a big job and that kind of pressure. The sum total sounds like *lonely*. Sure, I wouldn't think twice about saying yes. But the thought of picking up and starting over is kind of scary."

Dick Wald, president of NBC News at the time, called me at home one morning and said I had the job but couldn't tell anyone. I called home. A week later, on a Friday, I signed off.

There wasn't a party to celebrate. I went home to pack; movers were coming in the morning. From the outside, my life looked remarkable, even enviable, but from where I stood, looking out my high-rise windows, those twinkling lights were as mysterious and distant as they had been when I'd started, almost 365 days before.

I spent my last night in Chicago alone with a box of Kentucky Fried Chicken and my cats. I still called them "Boy Kitty" and "Girl Kitty." As a little girl, I'd named a Ginny doll "Ginny," a Revlon doll "Revvie," and a Betsy Wetsy "Betsy." Would my cats ever get names? Would I ever get a real life?

Before I could move on, I had to acknowledge the truth: I hadn't proved my critics wrong; I'd just outlasted them. I cried a little for the first time. It was so sad.

Tom Brokaw took me to dinner the night before our TV partnership officially began. I let him do most of the talking. What did I have to say that couldn't be summed up in a cartoon bubble over my head with an exclamation point?

We went to a popular new restaurant at the bottom of Fifth Avenue near Washington Square. I concentrated on looking casual while I pretended to eat my meal and Tom talked. He was new in town too, but I've never seen a city or a country or a situation that intimidated Tom Brokaw. He knows his way around. I have a theory that seeds of ambition planted in the most remote corners are unusually hardy—places like Hope, Arkansas, or Yankton, South Dakota, where Tom was born. Tom's family didn't have a TV until he was fifteen. By the time he figured out how big the world was, he was ready to own it. One thing we had in common, and that we'd later find we shared with Bill Clinton, is that we'd each been governors of Boys'/Girls' State. Each of us had exceeded our parents' expectations and on some level probably expected to. The difference is that Tom was self-made, without any lingering self-doubt. There was no question that he was driven—that's how he got to Los Angeles, where he was covering some of the stories I was giving extemporaneous speeches about in high school.

At dinner, he talked mostly about his family, which made me melt. What I most remember is how he used the word *devoted* like I'd never heard it used before. He said he and his wife, Meredith, "were devoted." He had it all. He was the father of three daughters, and I began to understand that while he was a "man's man," he didn't live in a man's world. This would have enormous practical benefits for me, and incalculable personal ones. The Brokaws folded me into their family at Thanksgiving, and Meredith began giving thought to my social life. When I returned to that restaurant, it would be with someone I would become likewise devoted to. He would talk about his family. I would melt.

But that night, on the way back uptown, Tom and I shared a Checker cab, and I held on to the strap as if my life depended on it. I had two cats and a tiger by the tail.

At about that time, the phrase "national malaise"—misattributed to Jimmy Carter—had earned the president the nickname Dr. Doom in the media. He was a glass–half–empty kind of person in a glass–half–full kind of country. In hindsight, I probably owe my career to our malaise. The country was tired, depressed, and ready for change.

I didn't read my press clippings—trained as I was to expect buried land mines. Even now, thumbing through three–ring binders that my very archival husband kept, I find that thirty–year–old clips are as lethal as when they were new. It's not only what was said about me—often it's what *I* said. When I'm at my best, I'm funny. When I'm funniest, it's at my own expense. But when I'm bad, I'm insufferable. I am stunned to see that in 1975, before I had even passed the Indianapolis city limits, I earnestly proclaimed: "I have worked hard at my craft!" My all–time low moment was saying something to the effect that "Jane Pauley is starting to be taken seriously."

Jane Pauley often talked about herself in the third person when she was taking herself most seriously.

• • •

Then there's the accent. I knew I was no Barbara Walters, but I alone didn't know that I was talking like her! People told me this constantly, and I would respond, "Why would I do that?" Until one morning before dawn, when I was standing alone in an Illinois barnyard waiting for the show to start, absentmindedly listening to tapes being logged, and I heard the voice of Barbara Walters! *What is she doing on the show?* I wondered, a little indignantly, and then sheepishly answered my own question. It was me! Watching a clip from *Today* on *Time and Again,* my daughter commented, "You sound like you're trying too hard, Mom." The irony was that I was trying so hard to be myself.

PART VI

Real Life

1976

It was amazing how quickly I felt like I fit right in, in New York. As soon as you declare your intention, you are a New Yorker. The first time I used a city bus, I noticed one of the passengers was Meryl Streep. I didn't let on that I knew, but as she got off by the back door where I was sitting, an older woman with her touched my arm and said, "Jane, I'm Meryl's mother-in-law, and I'm from Indianapolis, too." I didn't own the town, but at least I was getting some traction. I had a home, and had Tom Brokaw to thank for it. My mother was happy to oblige and told a reporter all about it— the corner, the color, the floor, everything but the address and my phone number.

Tom Brokaw had put me in the hands of a top real estate agent, who didn't normally deal in rentals. But she found me a two-bedroom, two-bathroom apartment, with a terrace, proximity to Central Park, and southern exposure. For years I made calculations along these lines: My rent was triple what I had paid in Indianapolis!

A postwar building, early sixties vintage, it was sheathed in brick—not red but blue. I had doubts about that. All the other buildings in the neighborhood were conventional colors—was I secure enough to stand out? I decided the building showed a sense of humor, and while a little odd, it was friendly and kind of sweet, which is exactly how I still thought of myself.

When I walked in my front door, I was welcomed by a happier view. This time my eye went straight outside to the terrace, partly because there was so little inside to look at. My glass dining table and six Breuer chairs—emergency purchases I had made when the family came to Chicago for Christmas—fit perfectly. I had my sofa bed and the "unfinished" desk I finished myself. I had my bed and brass headboard, a single nightstand (why only one?), and a matching bachelor's chest that I found at the Merchandise Mart in Chicago. I hadn't made any mistakes yet, but it was pretty sparse, and I knew nothing about decorating. This time, Meredith Brokaw stepped in.

Meredith volunteered a friend, Ellen, who had helped with her new apartment. Ellen guided me to very grown-up choices: a custom sofa and two slipper chairs, a parson's table in a maple veneer, and a Persian rug—old but not antique—that would one day go off to college with the twins I probably should have named "Tom" and "Meredith."

I was starting to accumulate possessions and become aware of life's amenities—like fresh flowers and votive candles, white wine with lunch, seafood. Who knew cheese came in more flavors than Baskin-Robbins ice cream? And so did olives! And coffee! Imagine being on the inside of Park Avenue apartments with private elevators and butlers who met you at the door. Imagine dinner parties where maids carried silver trays and wore black-and-white uniforms like in old movies. I never learned how to "circulate," so if I found someone to talk to, we would be sure to have exhausted our repertoire at cocktails, only to discover we were seated together for dinner, too. Imagine a candlelit dining room with three separate mahogany tables seating ten. Each place set with a dozen implements, on both sides and on top, and glasses galore; how is it I hadn't learned how to eat? When I was fourteen, I was sent to a "leadership" conference at Indiana University, where I was the youngest delegate. An etiquette expert gave a lecture, and I was seated next to him at dinner. He leaned close to say something: "You're eating my salad." I have never recovered.

Imagine, the haunt of Holden Caulfield in *The Catcher in the Rye*—Central Park, most famous for muggings. What a revelation! People went there! They strolled, played baseball, had picnics. Nearby was the reflecting pool where children and rich grandfathers floated motorized yachts. Weekends, lost in a crowd in the park, it was a pleasure to be alone with a book. I remember a particular Saturday and a particular book, *Black Orchid*, about a Jazz Age figure. It was tragic, of course, and perfect for reading in the old un-rehabilitated Central Park Zoo. The animals were all insane. It's okay to feel "poetically" alone; romance may be around the corner.

February 1977

I had seen Garry briefly once when he came to meet Tom at the studio—they were traveling to Washington together for the funeral of a mutual friend. As Tom later recalled, meeting at the studio hadn't been completely necessary. I caught only a fleeting glimpse of Garry then, but the first thing I would notice when we next met were his soft, kind eyes and his hair—but I could fix that.

On February 9, 1977, the Brokaws invited both of us to a dinner party. Garry and I quickly discovered that we had a lot in common: We had each upgraded the inventory of our freezers from Morton chicken potpies to Stouffer's frozen dinners. We shared a cab home, and the next day I waited for him to call. He didn't. Or the next day. Or the next. When a week passed, I decided to stop waiting. I sat on my bed, heaved a deep sigh, and just as I thought, *Well, I guess he's never going to call*—

BRRRIIINNNNNG.

I was literally looking at the phone when it rang. I recently asked Garry why he hadn't asked for my phone number in the cab. "Too shy," he replied.

Why didn't you call me right away?

"That was a double head-fake," he explained. He didn't want to ask Tom for my number too quickly.

On February 17, having purchased a large ficus tree for the occasion, to fill out some of the empty space in my apartment, I put my Willie Nelson record on. Because I wanted "Stardust" to be playing when Garry arrived, I had to pick up the needle and drop it at that cut over and over. Garry was late.

He decided at the last minute that his restaurant selection was "too romantic" for a first date, so he went to the phone booth on my corner and made a new reservation at that same restaurant Tom had taken me to four months before—which, considering the tens of thousands of restaurants in New York City, was interesting. It was not romantic, it was loud—even for a New York restaurant. And because he had a cold and couldn't hear anything I said, he elected to do all the talking, while I again pretended to be casual. He told me about taking his father on a fishing trip to Alaska. I left in love, and he left thinking that Jane Pauley was a really good listener.

"Wholesome, Midwestern, fresh-faced"—it was easy for the press to categorize me, but my relationship with Garry Trudeau threw some reporters, especially the younger ones. A girl even younger than I was said everyone in her Philadelphia newsroom wanted to know "If Garry Trudeau is so hip, why's he dating you?" I pretended I didn't follow the question and asked her to repeat it, but she lost her nerve. The day Garry and I first appeared in boldface together, I happened to be having a lunch interview for Frank Rich's piece for *Rolling Stone*. My fans were not legion among its readership—no baby boomer had yet turned thirty—but editor in chief Jann Wenner was always in tune with the zeitgeist, and I was part of it.

Garry brought civilization to my life. The first gift he gave me was a wastebasket (I used paper bags), and the second was a paring knife. He taught me the proper way to open an English muffin ("Not a knife! A fork!"). He even saw that the cats got proper names: the boy was Meatball and the girl Skitty—a play on skittish; she was a troubled thing.

Some kids are "sticky at the transitions," I heard a pediatrician say once. Though I didn't then make a connection to myself, I am a poster child for this, a little girl who gets a little lost when she feels alone in the world and who keeps wanting to go home. Getting traction in a new situation can be slow and hard when you're sticky at the transitions. And what is life but a series of transitions?

1978

You can get to know a person spending two hours a day sequestered in a studio together. One morning during a break, Tom Brokaw turned to me and casually asked what I weighed. I was so surprised, I remember both the question and the answer: 112 pounds. When Tom had asked on the air, musing about travel, "If you could be anywhere in the world, where would it be?" I had said, reflexively, "Panama City, Florida," which was not the answer he expected!

When I was growing up, I had traveled a lot compared to most of my friends. My father didn't consider a backyard barbecue worthy of a vacation. We packed up the car and went places. I'd seen a lot of the country east of the Mississippi. But I hadn't seen the world, or even dreamed of it. I wanted to be in some Panama City of my mind, with my family, like we used to be. I wanted to be home.

Things weren't like they used to be.

Like many long-married couples whose emotional lives become deeply enmeshed, my parents sometimes got on each other's nerves. Their personalities were changing in some ways

that I later recognized in myself when menopause arrived. It's acknowledged that women change, but men do, too. My father
could be impulsive, his judgment sometimes questionable; my
mother was more apt than before to question it. Her mild temperament took on a sharper, strident edge. He chafed against her
interference. Their marriage was never in danger, but they were.
There was a third factor, an invisible element, and it was driving
them to the brink.

Ann and I had seen it coming long before we knew what it
was. I had buried that bad memory of the celebration that wasn't
much of a celebration when I got the job at WMAQ. It was an
aberration, I thought, and nothing more. There were other subtle
signs that Daddy was different—the dinner in the restaurant in
Chicago, for instance, when he wasn't his usual self with the
waiter. I had buried that odd episode at a roadhouse: was Daddy
in a fight with Uncle Henry, or were they just fooling around? But
the signs began to be less subtle and more disturbing. He didn't
sound like himself on the telephone. He was slurring his words. I
was twenty-seven and Ann was thirty when we went home to
investigate. He picked us up at the airport.

We were on an interstate highway going home, Daddy at the
wheel, of course, doing seventy miles an hour as usual, when he
swerved sharply into the left lane in front of an oncoming truck.
Both Ann and I screamed. He seemed to have done it on purpose,
as if he'd been dueling with the other guy. We were terrified; it lent
urgency to our mission, though we still didn't suspect what the
trouble was. Later that evening, Ann noticed him heading down to
the basement, where he kept an office, and when he came up
again, he was obviously impaired. She went to investigate.

The evidence was hidden in plain sight; maybe it always had
been. There were vodka bottles behind his desk, and more in the
garage. The enormity of the discovery, and its impact on our
sense of family, cannot be described.

Alcohol wasn't served in our home; there was no alcohol in the house. So we thought. The father I knew didn't drink. How had he fooled us so utterly, so completely? It was obvious that my idea of us as a family had been based upon major misconceptions, but all of that was pushed way to the back, superseded by the urgency of the present moment—Daddy was in terrible trouble and, in the car, an immediate danger to our mother.

If there was a moment when my childhood ended and my adulthood began, that was it. Daddy's "little ol' Janie" stepped out of the way. Thereafter, whenever "Jane" stepped in, things happened.

I knew what had to be done but recognized that Ann was the better one to get him to do it; we agreed that she would speak to Daddy alone, because she wasn't as confrontational.

First, both of us talked to our mother. She took the news with quiet resignation. She was experienced at getting bad news. She didn't seem shocked by our revelation; she knew he drank, if not how much. She was willing to let us take charge, though in subsequent days, after we left, she vacillated between questioning whether he really had a serious drinking problem and being furious when he showed obvious signs of intoxication. I was so focused on his crisis and on lining up her support for our plan to get him into rehabilitation, I didn't think about the fact that he hadn't been alone in his "secret." And how both of my parents' lives must have been organized around the fact, acknowledged or not, of his drinking. She had aspired to be a missionary or homemaker when she was eighteen. Well, maybe she was both.

Of course, my mother's true calling was looking after my father. He was already a wounded bird when she declared her intention of marrying him. I don't think she noticed he was slipping away into alcohol until he was dangerously out of her reach.

When he started including her in his pattern of drinking, mixing them each a "frisky Fresca" instead of secretly spiking a Coke, alcohol had taken up residence at home. He perceived himself to be the same responsible married man all along, not calibrating the emotional distance between himself sober and himself not sober.

He may or may not have been "drunk," but he was not sober.

Disoriented as we were, Ann and I skipped right over denial: Daddy had a serious problem (though we remained in utter denial that it had, or would have had, any effect on *us*). I took for granted that I had the resources of NBC at my service, but ultimately it was Garry's family who came to the rescue.

Garry was already beloved by my parents, and after fifteen months of our being together was the presumptive fiancé, the "boyfriend–in–law." I was pretty comfortable about my future spot in his family, too. His father, Dr. Francis Trudeau, was my biggest fan, even if he rarely watched TV. One of Garry's uncles was a recovered alcoholic of twenty years. He once flew to Paris for A.A., to rescue a man he didn't even know. He told me about the Caron Foundation in Pennsylvania; there was a place for Daddy at the rehabilitation center known as Chit Chat.

Ann had the tougher job. She had been surprisingly confrontational. Reminding Daddy of the episode with the semi-trailer when he nearly got us killed, she threatened to take whatever steps were necessary to protect our mother. He listened to her and he didn't put up a fight. He was too sweet for that; he just was not able to acknowledge a drinking "problem."

Back in New York, I engaged in some long–distance crisis intervention. I was a nonstop fount of arguments, the legacy of high school debating. Daddy had an answer for every one. I was making no headway; he was wearing me down. Then I made a remark that seemed to cause a chemical reaction; it just spontaneously cleared the air. What I said was, "I know Mom can be difficult." My mother was hardly a shrew, and he was devoted to her, but she "could be critical" is the way he would have explained it. Why my acknowledgment had such an effect, I will never know. Perhaps it gave him permission to be angry at the woman he loved. For whatever reason, his attitude changed, and within a moment or two he said, "Well, if you girls think it's that important, I guess I'll go."

Ann delivered him to Pennsylvania days later. She sat with him in a waiting room, until someone came to lead him into another room beyond a door that wouldn't be opening again soon. He turned to look at her with tears in his eyes.

Daddy met some very nice people at Chit Chat—sweet, responsible gentlemen and women, not the "bums" that he associated with alcoholism. There was a celebrity; he said she was very kind. But he was confident down to his bones that he was not an alcoholic. I doubt he ever said, "My name is Dick and I'm an alcoholic." He was surely the toughest nut they never cracked. He never faced the truth, though he had faced truths far worse. But you'll find no hint of them in the autobiography he had to write at Chit Chat. He wrote that it was the story of "a dishonest man" who let everyone believe he was an "abstainer when he was not." The word *alcoholic* is not mentioned. But he reports that his drinking began on that ten-day excursion to Mexico in the summer of 1941. In his autobiography he is silent about the death of his parents, and the accident.

Almost immediately after returning sober from a month in Pennsylvania, he was hospitalized and near death—hemorrhaging, his damaged liver failing. A father-son team of surgeons discussed his options. The father thought Daddy could not survive surgery and would likely be a "vegetable" if he did. The younger man was more optimistic. But he warned that a consequence of a surgical bypass around the damaged part of his liver would be a buildup of residue in the brain and the possibility of mental impairment. We decided to give the surgery a chance—if he stopped hemorrhaging long enough for it to be performed. Fifteen years later, when Daddy was again near death, my father-in-law, Dr. Trudeau, told me that a man whose liver had been in the condition Daddy's was in 1978 would generally be expected to live for one year.

My father's remarkable resiliency was what enabled him to go on after he lost his mother so violently and so young. It enabled him to bury his first baby and yet imagine Mary "back in that maternity dress in no time." But nobody is that strong without a crutch. Alcohol was his emotional crutch, and it broke under the weight of too many burdens and too many years. However, resilience was there for him again when he recovered his strength. It would be there for my mother, too, when she needed him. And though he remained in denial about alcoholism for the rest of his life, he remained sober.

Ann and I were not in denial about it.

Well, yes we were.

During the surgery, we seemed to be losing Daddy. But he woke up one morning improved, remembering that an angel had been with him in the room. Ann had spent the night fearing the worst. He continued to mend, but day after day he seemed so depressed that I wondered if he wanted to go on. I had been there one morning, but when I came back in the afternoon, he wasn't in his bed. I found him smiling, getting some exercise in the corridor. Once they had taken out the catheter, he was anxious to live again!

His physical recovery was a marvel—though he was an older, slower man. Mentally he was himself again, but his judgment was suspect. He had liked long-haul drives—fourteen hours to Panama City, Florida—on coffee and catnaps. He had every intention of resuming his routine, in defiance of all the women who now ruled his life. His pride had taken a beating, but our threats prevailed, and he now made the drive in two days. We had been staying at the Holiday Inn on the beach since I was fourteen. After I put Panama City on the top of my dream list on *Today*, my parents had become VIP guests there, arriving to find WELCOME, JANE PAULEY'S PARENTS on a sign out front. A newspaper reporter dropped by to find them in residence, along with hundreds of drunken college kids on spring break.

Daddy loved his long, long solitary walks on the beach and started hooking rugs for something to do; I don't know what my mother did, but she enjoyed it there, too. Three weeks in a hotel room struck me as a little grim, so that's when I started renovating my parents. I bought them a condo. Daddy didn't ask for it, but it meant that at least his neighbors weren't fraternity boys. He was the most neighborly person I ever knew, and he made friends easily. He would say, "It's so nice to *greet* you." When Ann and I came for a visit, it was important we make the rounds and greet everyone, but my *Today* celebrity was a special premium. Walking the beach with Ann, I was surprised to hear myself say, "I feel like I don't have a father anymore. I'm just a visiting dignitary." After a short silence, I amended the statement, "But that's okay, I feel lucky to still have a father."

June 1980

"Today we found a house. I guess that means we can get married."

Garry's journal was lying open by the phone, so it wasn't like I was snooping. Besides I had "guest privileges": I could submit a vignette from a vacation, for instance. And it wasn't as personal as a diary. Later entries, for the latter part of June 1980, for example, list the restaurants we loved best in Paris but nothing about the event that took us to Paris—our honeymoon.

We were married at the house, outdoors. Our wedding was small and simple—no fuss. For example, I tried on three dresses and picked one. A week before the wedding, a hot water pipe burst in the kitchen and the ceiling caved in, but not before a steady stream of water drilled a hole through the Bible where we'd stashed bits and pieces of our ceremony.

Our first post-wedding stop was Dunkin' Donuts. By plan, the honeymoon to Paris was delayed a day because Garry had a *Doonesbury* deadline to meet. Sunday evening we were packed and ready to go when I heard him say, "I'd better check my passport.... Uh oh." Our trip to Paris was delayed another day, so we went to the movies instead. We saw *Star Wars: The Empire Strikes Back.*

In 1980, Alan Alda was offered Tom Brokaw's job—he declined. And while I got married and honeymooned in Paris, my putative replacement, Mariette Hartley, was given a tryout for mine. "Nobody's job is safe in television," *Time* declared in an article about the competition on morning TV. And nobody came out unscathed in the article, either. David Hartman's ego was "enormous," and Joan Lunden suffered one of the bitterest salvos from an "unnamed" colleague since I got hit in Chicago with the cantaloupe: "If you told her to jump off the Brooklyn Bridge she'd ask what time she should be there and what time the limo would pick her up afterward." Not even Tom Brokaw got off free—questioned about his "frosty demeanor," he responded unapologetically, "When you try to be something you are not, it will show through." Of me, it was sometimes said that Pauley "does not work hard enough."

• • •

In Sunday school we used to sing a self-evident song about building a house upon a rock instead of sand. Rockefeller Plaza is built of Indiana limestone. NBC is known in the industry as 30 Rock. My career, however, seemed to stand on a foundation less stable than shifting sand: luck.

Daddy/Jane

My trajectory is going up as steeply as Daddy's is going down
dramatically
His career is in the basement/I'm on TV
I'm famous/he's in A.A.
I find Garry/he loses Mary
I buy a condo/he sells the house
I have a housekeeper/he refuses help
I'm a mother/he has babysitters
I'm a world traveler/he's a shut-in
I try to be "just Janie"/he wants "Jane Pauley" to say hello . . .
I want to buy him stuff/he doesn't want stuff
I stop smoking/he stops drinking
I'm the loved one/I'm Pain

I was flattered when Garry said, "You've come a long way from that person I used to know," meaning that I was more able to recognize and respect my strengths. He had always loved my sense of humor, but my self-deprecating charm eluded him. He was the first guy who called me Jane, not Janie.

Summer 1981

The morning of the royal wedding of Prince Charles and Diana, in London in 1981, I told Tom Brokaw my secret: I was pregnant. Not quite three months. We hadn't told anyone outside the family, but given the part Tom had played in making us a family, he qualified. My motive for telling him then had to do with morning sickness and the prospect of the five-hour broadcast ahead of us that day. But as we now know, the royal wedding was fated to be a mismatched marriage, and my pregnancy would soon end in miscarriage. When I finally felt safe to tell the *Today* staff I was pregnant, I probably wasn't anymore. Before I found that out, our enterprising news rep had alerted the media. *Time* and *Newsweek* reported our pregnancy, and one week later, the miscarriage.

As a result, I got hundreds of letters from viewers—they were a surprising comfort. I found myself skipping to the bottom, where many of them said "…and now she's five years old." Or "…two boys and a girl!" After a miscarriage you feel certain you never will have another chance. It took a third time to be a charm. The technician doing our ultrasound said, "I hope you have a big house!" Garry didn't get it at first. We were having twins!

I told the boss, Steve Friedman, right away, because I didn't know what to expect, carrying twins, and again, it was a morning television show—a *live* morning show. I could imagine fleeing the studio inexplicably. But after my first miscarriage, Steve had showed up at the hospital, unannounced and unexpected, with flowers—not a lot of guys would do that. He was special.

After my first miscarriage, there had also been a second, so now, even after it was deemed safe to tell, I tried to be as low-key as a woman carrying twins and in close proximity to Willard Scott could possibly be. As soon as my first trimester passed safely, it seemed all right to tell what was becoming absurdly obvious. There was nothing subtle about carrying twins and nothing subtle about Willard: "We've got twice as many babies coming as any other morning show!" It was summer 1983.

One of the trade magazines speculated on the effect my condition would have on the morning race: "Given the premium the morning shows place on continuity, that redirected attention of gossipmongers to Pauley's maternity-leave (or permanent) replacement." *Today* was flirting with third place—CBS was making a run at us.

By the thirty-eighth week, I weighed 172 pounds, and I'd grown so weary and impatient that every time the phone rang, I thought it was the hospital calling to say, "It's time." Except for the doctor's visits, I was housebound. I had outgrown all the shoes in the house but Garry's and wore furry house slippers that had been a gag gift—mice, with big pink ears and long tails. Resigned to waiting forever, I kicked off the mice, hauled myself onto the bed, looked at the phone with a heavy sigh, and opened a book—*My Ántonia*.

Then I felt something. As a rookie, I didn't know whether this was it or only wishful thinking. That morning the doctor had checked me out and said, "Not today." But he hadn't ruled out "tonight." It was eight o'clock—curtains were rising on Broadway as we headed across town in a cab with bad shocks. Two new native New Yorkers were getting ready for their grand entrance: showtime!

The first act was a little slow. Contractions were inconclusive for a while. At around eleven o'clock, the pace quickened. Garry was doing his best to keep me focused on the red dot he'd stuck to the wall above the clock. Both of us were doing the special breathing we'd practiced—once or twice. It did nothing to improve the pain or my feelings for Garry, who valiantly took my abuse. But if it did nothing more than make the daddy a part of the process, that was probably enough. It also helped me focus on something other than my private earthquake.

The doctor dropped in to check the graph paper and said that my contractions were building impressively to "triple peaks." They felt that way, too—like tectonic plates pushing up against the ragged edge of the Alps. The spasms would rise, fall a little, rise even higher, then pause to regather for the topper. The kindly, silver-haired doctor was a calming presence. He said, "It won't get any worse," which was surprisingly reassuring.

He wasn't telling me everything, though. A nurse arrived to slip a tiny tube into the vein of my pudgy right hand, to hook up an intravenous drip. Later, she returned and asked me to turn and face the wall—a process that would have required a winch and a crane had I not been highly motivated to comply. She was holding the longest needle in the world, but it was my friend. Sometime after six A.M., they wheeled me into the arena.

The impending birth of my babies drew a small crowd to the delivery room. They weren't drawn by my celebrity but by the doctor's reputation. He was an old hand, and many young residents had never seen twins delivered vaginally. I didn't care. After ten hours, I was just anxious to get the show on the road. They might have been choirs of angels for the majesty of the morning light pouring in through the tall windows overlooking the East River. After hours of labor in a dim, windowless room, I found the delivery room afire in the red-gold light of a December dawn. Though I could feel nothing below my waist, a baby had arrived.

I could hear him crying. It didn't seem odd to be attached to an IV. I was almost relaxed, but there seemed to be some urgency about the second baby. I was commanded to "PUSH!!!" An epidural had numbed my lower parts, so I couldn't feel anything. I just clenched my jaw and used the think method. Somebody praised my effort, but it wasn't enough, because a nurse laid her forearm across my upper abdomen and pushed down; suddenly her arm was replaced by a more muscular, hairier arm, which seemed to be trying to squeeze the baby out of me like toothpaste from a tube. He cracked a rib.

Four minutes after the first baby arrived red with rage, Garry saw the second baby born—limp and blue, with the umbilical cord looped around her neck.

Yet within a minute, the baby girl was the APGAR equivalent of a perfect ten—pretty, pink, and serene. First they handed me my son. My arms were weak and shaking so hard I wondered if that was such a good idea. He did not have a hair on his large, shiny head, but he had deep, intelligent blue eyes. He'd had such a long, hard night—he needed a nap and he needed a mother. I signed right up.

Then I discovered my daughter, and she was breathtaking: a small, oval head with a faint aura of brown peach fuzz, red lips like a rosebud, dark eyes, serene and enigmatic. I didn't know how close we'd come to losing her, but Garry did. He also knew that I was the one in danger now. They wheeled me straight to intensive care—I was at risk of a stroke. After a completely normal pregnancy, my blood pressure skyrocketed during labor—hence the Valium drip—and it didn't come down to normal for three days.

*With Tom Brokaw and Ardeshir Zahedi, former Iranian ambassador
to the United States and adviser to the shah.*

At the Today *show anniversary party, with Dave Garroway and Hugh Downs.*

Ann and me on the Orient Express.

My parents, 1979.

Ann, Daddy, and me.
Garry's sister, Jeanne Fenn, took the picture.

On our wedding day, June 14, 1980.

At our wedding, with my father-in-law,
Dr. Francis B. Trudeau.

My parents in Panama City, Florida.

Cast of the Today *show:*
(left to right) Gene Shalit, Bryant Gumbel, Willard Scott, me, and John Palmer.

*On location for the Today show
with Bryant Gumbel;
we broadcast from the
Spanish Steps in Rome (left).*

*With the twins just after their birth in 1983,
photographed by Jill Krementz.*

Ross and Rickie visit Today *after the show.*

With Bryant Gumbel and
Willard Scott on the cruise ship
Norway, while pregnant
with Tom.

With Bryant on the
aircraft carrier Coral Sea.

On a family vacation.

*With my husband, Garry Trudeau,
in Paris on Bastille Day, July 1989.*

*Walking with Barbara Walters and
Barbara's daughter, Jacqueline, on Long Island.*

Stone Phillips and me
after we taped my last Dateline *show.*

Tom Brokaw and me.

My children, Rickie, Tom, and Ross.

In the first twenty-four hours, I spent one hour with my babies—I was limited to two thirty-minute visits. The following night, New Year's Eve, I was in a regular room with a window overlooking the river. Garry arrived with a large bag full of baby supplies. Impressed, I asked how he knew what to get; he said he just took everything with BABY on the label. We felt pretty smug at feeding time, when the nurses delivered newborns and the other new parents on the floor only got one. Our tiny babies were wheeled in fresh and clean and hungry several times a day. Garry took little Twin A and I took little Twin B. Or vice versa. It was the happiest New Year's Eve of my life, though to be honest, I'm not a fan of New Year's, so better to say it was the happiest day of my life. Exactly two years later on New Year's Eve, a glass of red wine was handed to me. Oddly, I couldn't drink it—I didn't even want to look at it. Our third child, my bonus baby, was born eight months later. He arrived quickly—no muss, no fuss, no epidural. Maybe it's a coincidence, but after his fourth Christmas this boy asked if I knew his favorite present. Here was his answer: "KITTW," which meant "koming into the world."

It would seem history can repeat itself. This time it all turns out right. A firstborn baby boy is healthy. And a baby with the umbilical cord around her neck is saved. The mother didn't have a stroke.

A postscript: I finished *My Ántonia* thirteen years after I started it, on my daughter's recommendation. Willa Cather was her favorite author.

When Steve Friedman took over *Today* in 1979, he didn't fire me, though he was urged to. He must have had second thoughts, because it took me so long to deliver the goods he thought I possessed. But I was transformed after the birth of the twins— or so I read. In her book *Inside Today*, Judy Kessler says that two successive presidents of CBS News "pinpoint the decline of *CBS*

Morning News and the surge of *Today* to Pauley's comeback. 'Pauley surprised us.... She returned a different persona.' " Not reading my own publicity, I didn't know I was being credited with turning the ratings around. *Today*'s ascendancy began in the spring and summer of 1984.

Conventional wisdom held that motherhood had made me "looser." It definitely made me happier. Personally, I don't rule out a placebo effect; perhaps as a consequence of this unprecedented new regard for me, I responded like a flower to the sun—I opened up.

Tom Brokaw, who left the *Today* show in 1982, had been orderly, but Bryant Gumbel, who succeeded him, was downright fastidious: His coordinating tie, socks, pen—and underwear!—were laid out every night. Even his notes were written out meticulously by hand, in ink that matched his ensemble. Nothing in his handsomely decorated office was random. I left behind chaos in the studio every morning—crumpled pages of script strewn about, scribbled notes, and newspapers tangled up under the wheels of my chair. We were an odd couple.

Bryant is older than I am and always will be, I like to say. He's no more than a year older, and what a difference that made. Tom was my big brother, but Bryant was just like a brother. I don't mean "just" a brother, because I really came to have a very soft spot for my partner, or my buddy, as he often refers to me. He's complicated. At the time, I was still under the impression that I was very uncomplicated, a straightforward Midwestern girl. I don't think Bryant found me that simple to understand.

It was at least a year—he says even longer—before our on-air relationship was really solid. There was a testing period. Despite my seniority, I didn't expect to be made host when Tom left, but I had to give it a shot. I made my case but lost. Bryant and I weren't equal in status—he was a host and I had a hyphen: co-host. I tacked a clever little statement about all the co-anchor hyphens in my résumé by saying, "Jane and her husband, Garry Trudeau, are co-parents of three children" at the bottom. Nobody got it, understandably.

Part of our success as an on-air team was based on the tension in the relationship—again, like brother and sister. Periodically, you have to mark your territory. I had no background in such sibling competition, having gone absolutely in the opposite direction with my sister—competition is dangerous; don't go there. Bryant didn't know that. He also didn't know that I have a weakness for vulnerable little boys—or the men they grow up to be—and he was one of them. Some people find Bryant strong medicine and can't understand my regard and loyalty. It goes back to something deep and emotional.

There were times I had to assume a better sibling relationship than was sometimes apparent. It was a situation I later encountered at home, when my youngest child, Tom, asked me what the definition of *faith* was. I must have said it was believing something you couldn't see or prove, because he said, "You mean like I have faith Ross [his big brother] loves me." Bryant and I had bonded, even if he did pay off a bet for a lobster dinner by having one flown in (overnight) and delivered to the studio at seven A.M.

Sometimes I felt on *Today* like Wendy in Never-Never Land with the Lost Boys. The show in those days had a reputation as a boys' club, and the rules were every man for himself. My assigned nickname, Lady Jane, conveys I was above the fray (and perhaps disengaged). But in Rio de Janeiro in a hotel overlooking the famous Copacabana, I found that my room overlooked the back of the hotel. What made this more irksome was noticing a pattern of room assignments for others that ended with the same numbers—the desirable rooms up and down the front of the hotel. Seeking an explanation, I learned that while lacking a view, my duplex had been a special consideration: Willard and I had each been assigned one of these rooms because they were "bigger" (I was pregnant at the time). On another occasion, I had the distinction of flying cross-country with four male colleagues in a four-seat private jet. I sat in the back in a seat that doubled as the john.

Thanks to *Today*, I have visited every hemisphere. I don't deserve any of it, because, given a choice, I would have missed it all! I would have chosen to stay home and never meet the pope once, much less three times. I learned how to say *good morning* in Polish and *twins* in Italian. Pope John Paul blessed a picture of my children.

The travel wasn't wasted on Garry, though he didn't always get to go. In Rome, he was alarmed to notice that our security guards seemed to be enjoying the show, so he put on sunglasses and pretended to look menacing. He was rewarded with a credit: Director of Security.

We were like skipping stones when we traveled—never alighting long enough to see much beyond the view out of hotel windows. Most of the Australians I met were delivering room service; they tended to be breathtakingly beautiful young people. In fact, most Australians are breathtakingly beautiful young people—it made being famous there so much fun! I had the TV on in my hotel room and kept hearing about "the duo" and realized they were referring to Bryant and me. In Australia, *Today* was a late-night TV phenomenon.

The Great Wall of China was built before the invention of private bathrooms, a revelation I had in a moment of some urgency. The explanation for my sudden disappearance was bounced by satellite around the world.

I returned from China to an angry little man. When I suggested to the twins that they pick up their toys, Ross said,
"You pick up the toys! Rickie and me go on a business trip!"

My ten-year-old daughter was fretting over a schoolmate. "I don't think she gets enough of her mommy," she said. Instinctively, I asked, "Do you ever feel like you don't get enough of Mommy?" Without hesitation, she said, "When I was five." We sat down right there on the kitchen floor and had a talk about it. I didn't have to do the math to know what year she was talking about.

Today, 1988–1989

We were a "family" of five—Bryant, Jane, Willard, John, and Gene. We didn't take one another home at night. We didn't do holidays and vacations. We didn't cry on one another's shoulders, counsel each other's kids, or babysit one another's dogs. But we had a rare thing going that clicked with viewers.

Rather than a boys' club, the show was more like a coed dorm—the cool one—and Bryant's room would have been the epicenter of everything: fun, food, and, occasionally, hurt feelings. As Garry put it, we had coagulated into a family.

But in 1988–1989, certain relationships had become strained after a confidential memo was lifted from Bryant's computer file and leaked to the press. My name wasn't mentioned in the memo, nor was I part of another spate of bad press that was whipped up into a feud between Bryant and David Letterman. The protracted public turmoil took a toll. *Today* was still the top-rated show in the morning, but our lead was softening, and with the competition hot on our heels, we had to run faster just to stay in one place—which translated into taking the show on the road more and more. It was the travel that weighed most heavily on me.

I had that other family at home—four-year-old twins and a toddler. And I had a guilty secret: At the sound of breaking news, I held my breath, hoping that the phone wouldn't ring.

When Boris Yeltsin climbed atop that tank in Moscow, NBC's Jane Pauley was sitting on the floor in front of the TV surrounded by tapered strips of newspaper, custom-designing a Morticia-style skirt for her daughter's Halloween costume.

News has been a part of my life from childhood, when my parents subscribed to three daily papers—and read them. Events had a way of leaping off the page and tapping them on their shoulders. I felt like I had a personal stake in the outcome of elections. Parents communicate these things to children, and/or it's a genetic trait. I certainly don't advocate feeding children the news every night—but my twin babies got their evening bottle during the *NBC Nightly News:* Garry fed one and I fed the other. When they were just two, and unrest in the Philippines was in the news night after night, Ross shoved his bottle aside and announced, "Marcos is bad man!" And when the *Challenger* explosion led the news for a month, after Bob Bazell signed off his story, Ross asked, "Where's Bob Hager?"

In thirteen years on *Today,* I probably traveled two hundred thousand miles. New Year's Day in 1988 was bleak because I knew I would have to get on so many planes that year, so I started worrying about it good and early. A presidential election year meant two conventions (Atlanta and New Orleans), and the Olympics basically meant September in Seoul. And a week on the Orient Express would be penciled in later. It sounds absurd—complaining about another trip to Europe.

Not that I was incapable of getting into the groove once things were under way: I have pictures that suggest someone was having a good time. On the Orient Express, I did the karaoke set

Judy Kessler wrote about in her book *Inside Today*—two Elvis standards and "Edelweiss"—sung while we were slipping through the Austrian Alps at sunset. Feeling a little sheepish about it later that night, I confided to Ann (who had come along and with whom I was sharing a compartment) that "I felt like I slept with fifty people."

"If it's any consolation," she said, "you'll wake up with your sister."

When another New Year came around, something wasn't right. I just didn't feel good. During a routine physical checkup, my insightful doctor asked, "Do you think you're a little depressed?"

"No," I said. And burst into tears.

Nobody knew, beyond family and a few friends who had noticed as I became more withdrawn. But the show was troubled, too, and even I didn't know that.

Paris 1989

Today planned a last-minute trip to Paris for the bicentennial of Bastille Day, July fourteenth. My travel dread was muted by the fact that Garry was coming along; it would be our first trip to Paris since our honeymoon nine years before. And it would be short: Only three days away from the kids, and then we would segue directly into our annual family vacation at Garry's boyhood home in the Adirondacks—my favorite week of the year. But while I was in unusually good spirits when we arrived at the Concorde waiting lounge at JFK Airport, everyone else seemed unusually subdued.

Today typically traveled with the savoir faire of a high school field trip. At first I attributed the difference to fatigue—we had just finished a show—or to the hauteur of the Air France personnel. But my antennae began to pick up other signals. Something was in the air, and there were people who were in the know and people who were out of it. If so, it was clear which group I belonged to.

I put it out of my mind; it was a wonderful trip. On Saturday night, Garry and I returned to a restaurant we remembered from our honeymoon, where we got more attention than we're accustomed to. We are typically seated by the kitchen door in restaurants all over the world, but here we were shown to a table overlooking the Seine. There were fireworks over Notre Dame Cathedral just across the river, as if for our exclusive enjoyment. Predictably, all I remember of the meal was dessert: spoonful after spoonful after spoonful after spoonful of rich, dark chocolate ladled over profiteroles. After that I wasn't sleepy, needless to say, so we decided to take a meandering stroll back to our hotel. Turning a corner, we came across a startling image on a giant TV screen set up in a public square. It was a bicentennial Bastille Day celebration being televised live all over the country. Hundreds of Parisians were enthralled by the towering image of a woman in a billowing yellow chiffon gown, her long black hair flowing in the breeze. I recognized the singer and the song. It was the "Marseillaise"—the French national anthem—and the singer was the great American soprano Jessye Norman. She was unforgettable; it was an unforgettable night.

The next morning was unforgettable, too. We joined some NBC friends for brunch before heading back to New York to scoop up the kids for the trip to Grandpa's house in the Adirondacks, so I was feeling very lucky. But Tim Russert, stopping me on our way out of the restaurant, had a long face as he pulled something out of his coat pocket. He showed me a story that was running on the wires about a change in management at NBC News. There was a new executive in charge of *Today*.

Now I recollected the mood in the waiting lounge of JFK. I had been right. Something was up, and some people had been in the loop and others were out of it. The expression on Tim's face suggested he was thinking what I was thinking. As *Time* magazine had reported almost ten years earlier, there is no such thing as job security in television. I was to discover there are worse things than losing your job—like *not* losing it.

On the long drive up the Northway to the Adirondacks, with my three babies asleep in the back of our minivan and Garry singing along to the radio, I remember turning my head as far to the right as I could, so that he wouldn't see the tears. I didn't know why I was so sad.... I was just so very, very sad.

Dick Ebersol, formerly of *Saturday Night Live*, was the wunderkind producer of his television generation—"as charming as he was slick" (*Inside Today*, Judy Kessler). Six-foot-four, dynamic, handsome, and married to TV star Susan Saint James, Ebersol was not unaccustomed to attention. Only that spring (1989), at forty-two, he had been named president of NBC Sports, having privately lobbied to have charge of *Today* as well. Four months later, over the vigorous private opposition of the top news figures, including Tom Brokaw and Tim Russert, who objected to a sports executive managing one of the jewels in the NBC News crown, it was a done deal.

While we had lingered over dinner in Paris that Saturday, the announcement was made in Los Angeles in a joint appearance by Dick Ebersol and Michael Gartner, then president of NBC News. Gartner expressed confidence in the partnership. Ebersol told the press that there were no plans for major changes, but before Labor Day, the face of *Today* had changed substantially.

While *Today* was still number one, the ratings dip was in the key demographic—women eighteen to thirty-four. Turning to a male sports executive might seem counterintuitive, but Ebersol had the hot hand.

July 1989

It was the thirtieth of July—two weeks since the news bulletin in Paris—and I was getting ready for a party at the home of Bob and Suzanne Wright. My social confidence is fragile at best. I will never have a wardrobe that bridges the gap between play clothes and school clothes. Rummaging around my closet for an hour produced nothing that said *clambake*. Reminding myself, *Nobody will be looking at you*, I headed to their home.

The Wrights are always wonderful hosts, but I arrived uncertain about more than my clothes. There was a large white tent set up on a sweeping lawn, along with twenty or so tables. I was grateful to be seated next to everybody's favorite television executive, Gordon Manning. His legendary Gord-o-grams were coveted for their wit and unpretentious erudition. I saved one that compliments me for this remark one morning on *Today*: "Paleontology: the study of prehistoric executives at CBS." I couldn't have enjoyed a better dinner partner. But I felt petty and mean for noticing who was sitting with the guest of honor, GE chairman Jack Welch.

I've never coveted a seat in the inner circle—my natural inclination is to cling to the walls—but there was nobody there that evening, ours being a news organization, who didn't take note of the table gilded in late summer sun where Jane and Jack Welch sat surrounded by animated young silhouettes—including Bryant Gumbel and Deborah Norville. Deborah, the attractive newcomer, had come from WMAQ-TV in Chicago, as I had a dozen years before.

Deborah's regular assignment was anchor of the early, early morning news program, *NBC News at Sunrise.* Her audience was small but significant, saturated with type-A executives, including the most important business executive in the world: Jack Welch, then fifty-three, who reportedly enjoyed her program while riding his exercise bike at the crack of dawn. While *Nightly News* had fallen into third place and *Today's* lock on number one was under assault, Deborah's show was a strong first place in its time period. If NBC didn't make Deborah happy, some other network would.

That summer I was taking most of my vacation time in long weekends with Garry and the kids. Deborah had been filling in for me pretty regularly. Because I back-loaded my vacation time, between July and August she appeared on *Today* almost as often as I did.

In August Dick came to my office to deliver personally belated but enthusiastic assurances that "great things" were in store. But this concerned me most of all. "Great things" for me meant even greater demands *on* me. With three small children at home, I couldn't kick it up another notch.

It soon became apparent that great things didn't include all of us. Within weeks, John Palmer departed without comment after the show on a Friday. On Monday he was sitting at the *Sunrise* desk, and Deborah Norville was the occupant of the *Today* news nook.

The first order of business was shooting a new *Today* family portrait.

I'd posed for countless cast photos—the only member of my original *Today* family who was still in this picture was Gene Shalit. Dick Ebersol appeared to have something specific in mind for this photo; he was in the studio, personally shifting us around and calling the shots. When he was finally satisfied, I told him that it looked to me like Bryant had acquired a new co-host. Dick denied there was any subtext to the photo and seemed hurt and surprised that I would even think that. I was pretty surprised that I had said it.

Some may take to fame like ducks to water, but as often as not, I just wanted to duck.

PART VII

It's Not About the Cat

Labor Day, 1989

Friday night of Labor Day weekend, we were expecting old friends for dinner at our summer house, leaving the cat unaccounted for in the city, where a renovation project was deep in the demolition stages. The rubble and dust were a perfect metaphor for my life—the happy chaos of old and new suited me fine. But the cat was traumatized by it, and there had been no sign of her—all morning, all afternoon, nothing. Fearing the worst, I drafted a friend to continue the search, but by evening she was still nowhere to be found. Thinking of windows left wide open so workmen could breathe, I imagined the worst. I started to cry just when our friends arrived—and I didn't stop. For hours I cried my heart out—for Daisy. Now and then I'd catch my breath and think, *Is this really about the cat?* Then I'd say, *Yes!* and cry some more.

Happily, Daisy turned up in our apartment the next morning, waiting for someone to feed her, and she lives still—fourteen years later. I like my cat a lot, but the episode was pretty strange. I assume there were some crossed wires. I needed a good cry, even if I didn't know why I was crying.

The day after Labor Day, September fifth, some people, including me, were surprised to see the three of us—Bryant, Deborah, and me—sitting together on the couch at the opening of the program. Dick had given me a heads-up that from time to time Deborah would be joining Bryant and me on the couch. But I didn't understand this to mean that it would be at the top of the show, until I looked up at the monitor and saw it! I told a reporter much later, "It was not so much who was sitting where as who was on camera when."

Tom Shales of *The Washington Post* wrote, "Watching the three of them on screen together is like looking at a broken marriage with the home-wrecker right there on the premises! Gumbel seems more comfortable now with Norville than with Pauley, and Norville sometimes has a self-satisfied smirk on her face. Like Eve in *All About Eve*."

Deborah took the heat. It was not her fault that I looked like I was being squeezed out of the picture, but by that point I was becoming more than ready to oblige.

On vacation I'd started taking an inventory of my life. My conclusion was that after thirteen years—a record for morning television—I'd overstayed my welcome. I was a placeholder. But I had two years to go on my contract. Two years is a long time to be somewhere you're not wanted. And even more than I realized, I was wanted at home. Above all, two years is a very long time in the life of small children. Sitting at my desk after I returned from my first maternity leave, I had posed a question to myself that I was never able to answer satisfactorily: *If I'm working full-time, am I a part-time mother?*

The scales were out of balance before Ebersol came on the scene. The factor that shoved me over the tipping point was not, as everyone presumed, the presence of an attractive younger woman; it was the expansion of the news anchor role. Deborah would be conducting "newsmaker interviews," a departure from tradition. And she was an assertive newswoman. The practical effect of this was that either my role would be diminished or that I could contend daily for airtime, which I was not prepared to do. I began to look for a third option.

With a signed contract, what choice did I have? It felt like my children were being held hostage to my career—and whose fault was that but my own?

The phrase "settle my contract" had not been part of my everyday vocabulary but had come from my agent, Ralph Mann, who remains one of the most respected names in the business. A founder of International Creative Management (ICM), he'd done thousands of deals and contracts, including all of mine since 1976, when we were introduced by Floyd Kalber. Of all Ralph's clients, I was probably the least likely to play hardball—I lacked the skill, the temperament, and the power to pull it off. When NBC News president Larry Grossman had said I was the sanest person in the business, or words to that effect, he might have been factoring that in.

Ralph had surely seen it all, but not from me. Now I was asking him to undo a deal. I doubt that many clients had asked him how to give the money back. Sitting in his handsome midtown office, always the total gentleman, he never pointed out that my request to settle the contract, in the event that NBC went along with it, left a dangling loose end—the fee he was legally entitled to for having negotiated the contract. Instead, he freely gave me his support, friendship, and legal counsel.

An associate at ICM who was called in to clarify for me the legal implications of the gesture I was contemplating looked stunned by the proposal. He made it plain to me that NBC could just say no. And while I wouldn't be the first disgruntled "talent" to pull a no-show, the company would be within its legal rights to come after me for breach of contract and ask for financial penalties far beyond the amount of the agreement I was seeking to terminate. I didn't expect the situation to become contentious. But I was prepared to pay a price. There were no terms, short of "You can't leave," that I would have considered too harsh. At a minimum, I expected to give up the remaining money and to agree not to work anywhere in television (or anywhere, period, if necessary) for the duration of the unfinished contract—or even longer. I envisioned a win/win scenario in which I would be given a warm send-off and in turn I would help launch a new generation of *Today*. Who wouldn't agree that my turn had been long enough?

Fortified by the conviction that my analysis was not flawed, I believed that the network would actually welcome getting out of our deal. In that case, I had nothing to lose and, thinking of my kids, a great deal to gain. Being a pretty good salesperson, I was convinced beyond a doubt that my powers of persuasion and goodwill would carry the day. I felt I had far less to lose by vanishing from TV altogether than from fading away.

I shared my thoughts with a widening circle of family and friends. With one exception, it was never easy. My father-in-law, Dr. Trudeau, barely needed an explanation. He was the person in my life least invested in celebrity. A busy doctor, up and out too early to watch *Today*, he saw me as the beloved but busy mother of his three grandchildren.

Telling my own father was much harder. To be so cavalier when money like that was involved, and so bold with senior executives, was incomprehensible to a man of his generation. Besides, how would he and my mother fill another two hours in the day? What a rare thing for a retired couple in Florida to turn on the TV five days a week and see how Janie is doing her hair this morning, and whether she looks tired or says something funny that someone will mention at the bank or at the supermarket. Mr. Pauley was a bit of a local celebrity.

I needed everyone to be on board, including, strangely, the children. "Do you think Mommy should quit working?" My daughter was jubilant at the prospect, while her brother simply looked confused. "Why would you do that?" he said. "I just want to be a good mommy," I replied. "You *are* a good mommy," he said.

I caught John Palmer just as he was going into the *Sunrise* studio, to tell him I was going to ask to settle my contract. I was surprised to see the blood drain from his face. He was about one minute from air, and it appeared to knock the wind out of his lungs. He still talks about it with awe.

I wonder if I would have to be a man to appreciate how gut-crazy or courageous that must have looked to him. I was a mother of three—he was a father of three—and with apparent ease, I was telling NBC that if they wanted to give the best job in television to somebody else, I could help. I just wanted to go home.

Around nine-thirty Thursday morning, September seventh—two days after the sofa threesome that the papers were still going on about—I pulled the trigger. I asked for a moment with Dick Ebersol, and he agreed to stop by my office after the show. When I told him what was on my mind, for just an instant he looked rather stunned. But quickly gathering his wits, he heard me out while searching my face for my real agenda. He had plenty of time. As my children grew, they would often ask a rhetorical question: "Is this going to be a long speech, Mom?"

By the time I met with Dick, I'd made that speech a dozen times, beginning with Garry and my sister, then various friends, including well-regarded associates in TV—refining my points, testing my arguments and my will. It always took about an hour and a half.

I never wrote it down or took notes, so after all these years all I remember are highlights. I told Dick, with examples, that whenever he gave me a heads–up it turned out to be less than the whole story and that when he told the press that "Jane signed off on everything," it supposed I had any other option. In other words, there had never been a foundation laid for a relationship of trust and cooperation. Since mid–July, I had felt less and less a member of the *Today* family. I had concluded that my services were of little genuine value—and that it would appear to be of mutual advantage to NBC and me if we quickly found a way to part amicably.

Everything in his experience as a television producer—which was considerable, though heavily weighted in a masculine direction—said that it's *always* about the money: *If she says she doesn't want the money, she means she wants more money.* Dick concluded that it was just a power play, and he said so. I was a little flattered that he thought I had the guts to try, but from my perspective, I had little power to play—maybe just enough to leverage leaving.

For the rest of September and through October, our little drama provoked the biggest media frenzy. Almost weekly, NBC president Michael Gartner and Dick Ebersol and Ralph Mann and I met behind closed doors—with about a million ears pressed against the door. There were no raised voices, tears, or press releases. Once the media arrived, they took their seats right up onstage and started rewriting the second act. The media abhors a vacuum and filled in the details with speculation—virtually all of it in my favor and most of it at Deborah's expense.

Deborah and I were told not to comment. We were like actors in a Kabuki play, going about our mornings, apparently insensible to the drama the audience could see unfolding around us.

Daily and sometimes even nightly, Deborah was being eviscerated, while I was being lionized. Did everyone wake up and realize how much they loved me? I'd like to think so, but I don't.

Because viewers had been strongly cued to identify change with Deborah, when it seemed abrupt, jarring, and threatening to the old-timers, she was the lightning rod for their displeasure.

Meanwhile, I was trying to make a quiet exit from the stage, and instead, I was becoming famous on a scale unprecedented in my career. But as weeks went by, my resolve to leave only got stronger. I felt stronger, too, confident that I would get that farewell party I wanted before the year was out.

Though the talks dragged on and on, I almost felt in control of my life again. I'm pretty comfortable with change as long as I'm making the call. For weeks, I had imagined how it would be not getting up at three-thirty in the morning for the first time since I was twenty-five.

The twins had just started kindergarten; my youngest had just turned three. Garry had developed some proprietary feelings about taking the kids to school. He enjoyed being the sole father in a sea of mothers, and he was a little worried about what kind of changes I'd be making. I enjoyed contemplating those changes. I imagined learning a foreign language in the morning—maybe alternating with piano lessons. I could take cooking lessons. All the usual fantasy stuff.

I had no mixed feelings about my decision. In the meantime, while waiting for my future to begin, it wasn't that hard getting up at three-thirty in the morning, and if anything, my daily performance on the show was as good as or better than ever, at least in my own estimation. But everything was contingent upon the settling of my contract.

But the network seemed equally resolute, though without animosity: We can't let you leave, you're too important to the company. In mid-October, a close adviser pointed out: "You don't seem to be prepared for anything but total victory." I shivered with the cold realization that NBC could not let me win. I realized for the first time that it wasn't about me, it was about the contract. To settle one contract would undermine all the other contracts. I finally got it.

The night I accepted the truth, I mourned the future I'd imagined, hostage to fame and fortune.

October 1989

After a night of anxiety, I woke up with Plan B. It was a completely unoriginal idea that at the time seemed like a stroke of genius! It happened that our weekly meeting was scheduled for later that day. As I waited for the car that very dark October morning, I scribbled down ideas, my fingers trying to keep up. When I stepped into the meeting, I had an outline written up and down the sides of the folder that morning's script had arrived in. I spoke first. "I have some ideas about things we might do together." With that, the room itself seemed to breathe a sigh of relief. The expression on the faces around the room all said, *She's back!* Indeed I was. And a member of the NBC News family, in surprisingly good standing.

Total victory would have meant I got to go home, where I was both needed and wanted. But in the end, it was another split decision. I could leave *Today,* but I couldn't go home. In fact, instead of settling my contract, I had to sign an extension to my contract. In other words, I lost. But it turned out that the change itself did me good.

The bottom line for the network was far less rosy. The *Today* ratings plunged. The following year, Deborah took maternity leave and did not return to *Today.* But in the years since, *Today* has soared to unprecedented heights in ratings and revenues. And Deborah returned in 2004 to the NBC family, with her own show on MSNBC.

Over the next fourteen years, NBC and I regularly renewed our vows privately, without fanfare. Though *Real Life with Jane Pauley* was NBC News's sixteenth failure in as many tries at a newsmagazine, it begat *Dateline*, and that was a different story entirely.

Dick Ebersol's fortunes exceeded mine. I'm reminded of a phrase Steve Friedman liked to use: "You gotta risk a three to get a ten." People who take chances are capable of colossal success—if they're willing to risk failure. Dick is just the kind of executive Jack Welch loved. Even if you put all the 1990 *Today* losses on his ledger, NBC comes out way ahead. That's why he's still president of NBC Sports.

Michael Gartner left the network in 1993, after the *Dateline* pickup truck scandal. I was the first person to call and wish him well.

Bryant Gumbel and I never spoke about this, during or after. I've seen it said that Bryant was not my biggest fan, that he had a hand in bringing Dick over. I don't really care. I love the guy and he loves me back. I've always said that one of us will be speaking at the other's funeral—if I go first, he'll be funnier.

I have to laugh when I recall how often I paraphrased Robert Burns—"Oh would that I had the gift He gives us/To see ourselves as others see us"—thirteen years ago, when I did *Real Life*. I was thinking of everyone else, not realizing I had yet to be given the gift myself. Who was that woman who in 1989 concluded that after thirteen years she was not part of NBC's strategic thinking;

who conceived a scenario by which she left and everyone would be happy; who pulled the trigger, negotiated on her own behalf, and when it wasn't going according to plan, conceived of a new one? It was me—I'd had the power all along.

Having been wedded to the qualities that made Janie such a delight—warmth, empathy, a self-deprecating sense of humor, and Hoosier humility—I had to admit this newly discovered (by me) persona was not that attractive. But this was the woman Garry had married. I was flattered when he said, "You've come a long way from that person I used to know."

A stylist once made an observation I wish she hadn't—that more people see you from the back than from the front. Not only do they see you from the back, they recognize you. I discovered that for myself when I saw a friend up ahead of me in the park wearing sweats and sneakers, a baseball cap, and sunglasses—the same outfit I had worn for years under the impression I was anonymous.

We spend so much effort working on our presentation in the bathroom mirror, as if the only people who see us exclusively from our most flattering aspects aren't ourselves. I have been thinking that the same observation applies to those qualities so unfamiliar to me but so recognizable to others, those strengths I discovered in that business book my sister gave me. They've been around a long time. I can speak with certitude sometimes, and my skills at debate are supported by my ability to see patterns and make connections that can overwhelm a dialogue. Only yesterday, I was told, "Sometimes you don't realize how powerful you are." I've heard it before.

My self-image still tilts toward the delightful little girl, but under certain circumstances, I'm fearless. Though I understood the gravity of my decision, it was no extraordinary act of courage for me to tell Dick Ebersol I wanted to settle my *Today* contract. I was flabbergasted when he called it a power play, because the way I saw it, a diva would demand more; I was only demanding *less.* If I appeared formidable on defense, it's because that's where I concentrated my strength.

Summer 2000

Feeling the winds of change, I want to follow them—wondering all over again: What do I want to be when I grow up?

What do you want?
Freedom.
From?
Pressure.
What kind of pressure?
To be something I'm not.
What are you not?
I'm not chomping at the bit.
Were you ever?
Not really.
So what's changed?
I noticed.
For the first time?
No—but it's first in line now.
Chomping at the bit—what's that mean anyway?
Eager, focused, passionate.

Obviously you're not. How is it possible you never were?

I had talent, I suppose.

You suppose?

How else to explain it?

Surely you were ambitious?

Guilty.

Guilty? Pretty conflicted about that ambition?

How can you be ambitious without . . . reaching out for the next rung? It felt like I was always getting a hand.

"Give her a hand" also means applause. You like applause.

Oh yes.

Did you think you deserved it?

Do you mean "do" I or "did" I?

Start with "did."

Yes.

Why?

Because there would have been no reason to applaud if I wasn't doing something worthy of it. And—we're talking about applause, not the Congressional Medal of Honor.

What do you mean, worthy?

A lot of people manage to get on camera—but not all are asked to stay, much less get applause.

What about "do" you still deserve it?

Yes and no. Yes because when called upon, I still do well what I was being applauded for. In fact, I've never been better. What I don't do well, however, are the off-camera parts. The chase, the hunt—the "get." I'd call it the "heavy lifting" stuff because it can be so hard for me to pick up a phone. Ironically, I might even have a talent for that—but it's anathema to me—so I come to it with heavy, heavy resistance.

That's what you're not chomping at the bit for, isn't it?

I'm not competitive enough.

Enough?

I'm very competitive in that losing is very hard—but my state of mind makes losing more likely, doesn't it?

I see what you mean. You get it coming and going.

What I don't know, however, is whether all of this is bogus.

Why would that be?

It's that coming and going you mentioned—I'm the one who finds a way to block all the exits. Some of this must be bogus.

For example?

Well—I'm thinking about that "felt like I was always getting a hand." What does that mean? The hand of *God*? A lucky hand? This is really clever when you think about it. I'm not "feeling" anything in a literal sense, only that gee-whiz sense that aid is arriving from the fourth dimension. It's out of *my* hands, so I cannot accept credit. The blame, however, that's all mine, evidently.

Does that mean you have to surrender, and quit?

It means I *want* to, not that I *have* to.

That's what surrender implies: "I give up."

Well . . . I haven't yet.

What's holding you back?

A contract first. And "giving up"—obviously, I'm not happy with that prospect.

What options do you have?

I could wait for that hand of God. Or the lucky hand, or the handsome prince.

The prince part—that's a metaphor for a fantasy you've had for a long time.

I noticed that, too. Yes . . . the Things Falling out of Heaven Theory. Out of the blue.

If you give up on a fantasy (now that you've named it), what's the reality in its place?

My own hands?

I thought depression was basically a poor lifestyle choice: a retreat, as real as my tummy aches in the first grade, when I wanted to stay home with Mommy.

Whenever I began a long interview for *Dateline*, I would typically assure a guest that as random as my questions appeared to be, it would all make sense in the end. Not only didn't I work from a numbered list of questions, I preferred to do an interview without notes, because that way I'd be free to follow the conversation where I hadn't planned for it to go—I'd be prepared for the unexpected. My method of preparation, unless a book was involved, generally began the night before, reading background notes, articles—homework. I learned that it was most effective for me to upload everything and sleep on it; then the next morning I could sit at my computer, and dozens of questions would be just waiting for me to download. I tried to organize them in meaningful clusters, but it didn't matter, because the questions came out in an order that was only apparent at the end.

My style of interview was like a helix—a circuitous route progressing to my destination. I rarely began with a preconceived notion of what the story was; it revealed itself along the way. I didn't regard this as a virtue, nor did the crews who endured my conversations, but I didn't see it as a crippling weakness. Here was the rare example of my making a weakness into a strength without ever battering myself for lacking the discipline of a trial lawyer in cross-examination. I even enjoyed it.

It was this style that differentiated me from my colleagues and competitors both. A more typical line of questioning was organized around a target. Even a savvy audience knew what the money question was. I'm afraid they would fall asleep waiting for me to ask it. A common critique of my work was: "Jane won't ask the hard questions." There was more truth to this than they knew—I'd never asked my father what happened to his mommy and daddy!

I tried to be careful with people, who, after all, had trusted me with their lives, so to speak: to translate their lives into a two-hour interview and then reduce that to a twelve-minute story on prime-time television. I'd often assure them, "We only use the good stuff." I could say that in good conscience as a journalist because I rarely interviewed scoundrels who didn't deserve the consideration. They were better left to interviewers who wouldn't give it. I loved seeing scoundrels exposed, but exposing them was neither my strength nor my passion, and I regularly underestimated how coolly some people could admit to shocking indiscretions. I sometimes made the mistake of presuming that everyone valued integrity over fame. The big ones often got away from me.

I never went for shocking revelations. For a veteran newswoman, this is itself a shocking admission. I looked for revelations that illuminated something about life, imagining that my guest learned something new from our conversation and that the viewer did, too—or maybe only I did. Whenever I am asked, "Who was your favorite interview?" my wires cross. I don't file interviews by name; you'll find them listed according to ideas. For instance, I had done a story about an amazing young man who despite profound dyslexia (he couldn't read a menu at Denny's) was enrolled at Yale Law School. His secret weapon was his gray-haired mother, who had been his reader since second grade. We had a shot of them working together in the middle of the night in the stacks at the law library—a time when they could talk and avoid disturbing other students. For an instant, the mother's eyes closed and she dozed. Thinking about that moment and the thousands of others before it, I asked her, "Aren't you weary?" She said, "But I don't come to it with resistance." That was when I realized I came to everything with resistance—everything but finding ideas like that one.

Appearing to be someone I knew I was not: Whether anyone else knew it or not . . . I did. That's one too many.

Some years ago, a women's magazine asked its readers how they coped with the "juggling act," and one wrote, "I stopped reading articles about Jane Pauley." I wondered if she had me confused with someone else.

I told one reporter, with pride, as the mother of one-year-old twins, that during a regular checkup the doctor had said I looked "drawn and weary," which I regarded as proof I must be doing something right. Yet, despite what I said—or even how I said it— something drew reporters irresistibly to the opposite conclusion.

"Something in her manner appears so intact, you assume her cupboards are neat and her closet organized."

"She sits as if a slouch were a physical impossibility; she speaks complete sentences in modulated tones; she pronounces all the T's and G's, as if any minute she'll pause for a brief commercial message."

This myth of my plastic perfection persisted year after year and women who could have taken comfort in their competence were deprived of the chance or, worse, were left feeling insufficient: They didn't have it all and couldn't do it all. And I was left fuming, because against all evidence, yet another reporter per-petuated the myth: "Even her cupboards are neat."

I was as put off by that phony supermom stuff as anyone else. One year I was honored in a Mother's Day poll right behind Bar-bara Bush. I might have taken it a little too literally, but I turned down a well-meant invitation to be a worthy organization's mother of the year, because they had scant knowledge of what kind of mother I was. I was probably thinking: Does a mother of the year employ a full-time nanny?

That's not how I was raised. On those rare evenings when my mom left the house without us, her mother's helper was an eighty-six-year-old woman from up the street who walked very, very slowly with a cane and personified her title: sitter. Not one mother on our block had a paid job until Mrs. Morrow started teaching, and by then her daughter Carol was probably old enough to babysit herself. Jane Falconbury, the lady next door, looked after the two daughters of the only working mother I knew—who was also the only mother I knew who wore as much makeup as I do now.

I had heard that a certain superstar mom did all her own ironing; I believed it, because she lived in my building briefly and called me to ask about "a good greengrocer" in the neigh-borhood (as if I knew). Not long ago, I heard the same woman say on TV that she doesn't cook. She was still a supermom in my book—not because she does it all, but because she does more than a woman in her position has to. She makes choices a star isn't expected to make—which is probably the basis for my own outsize image. A celebrity mom who appears to be interested in her kids gets bonus points, just like any modern father who does more than his own dad did—because both he and the celebrity mom are perceived as making choices they don't have to. Ironi-cally, my best accomplishment as a celebrity mother was keeping the media out of my children's lives, though my daughter would beg to differ. She has accused me of being a "bad celebrity."

When the phrase "the get" was coined, the focus of my job shifted. Pursuing stories became almost as important as telling them. My job was to land the big newsmaker interviews. The ratings spiked whenever a newsmagazine bagged one of these trophies. I was not cut out to be a big-game hunter.

It went against my grain in every possible way. Imposing myself upon a person; intruding in a moment of crisis, without an introduction or an invitation; trying to persuade someone that a TV interview was in his best interest, when I didn't always think it was; and cold-calling at an inopportune moment—this is all material of core resistance for me.

To crash a party or to drop my name or to dial an unlisted number—whether it's due to genetics or upbringing, it's just not in my makeup.

I was the wrong bird.

Clearwater, Florida

In the spring of 1983, we lost the mother we knew. It was a Sunday, and Ann and I had just left Indianapolis after a really pleasant weekend. Mom had seemed in good spirits—it was a notable change. After we left, Daddy later told us, he had started talking about driving down to Florida. She demurred. He insisted and even threatened to go with or without her. She was terribly upset, and later that day she collapsed with a stroke. He blamed himself.

Mom suffered irreparable damage: Her speech was affected, and her memory. She could walk with assistance, but the nerves on the left side of her face and her left arm and leg were permanently damaged. We had lost our mother in a meaningful sense. But we were so lucky—she was not gone, so there was no reason to grieve.

Daddy waited years for signs of improvement, but my mother was an invalid now, dependent on him for everything, including all of her personal needs. He cooked, cleaned, and cared for her, alone, twenty-four hours a day. His wedding vows had an "in sickness and in health" clause, and he was a strict constructionist. For years, family and friends told him, "Dick, get

some help!" He always said, "What would people say?" The people who would judge him were all in his own head, a committee
that held him personally responsible for her condition.

I tried to renovate my parents. Daddy submitted to my hair-
cuts because they were free and Mom to perms because she liked
being pampered. Her gnarled fingers got a manicure while the
news simmered on CNN hour after hour. She hardly got out, yet
I brought her designer-label knit suits—he put them in the
washing machine. I slipped a new nightgown and underwear
from JC Penney into her drawer—he put a check in the mail. The
only thing he hated more than spending his own money was me
spending mine.

But I bought them a better condo. Worried about their access
to a hospital and my access to them, I was inspired to move them
to Clearwater, Florida, where Daddy happened to have a cousin in
real estate. I looked at a garden apartment, and I owned it three
days later. Now he had family nearby, his daughters were only a
direct flight away, and a good hospital was just three minutes
away! He didn't put up much of a fight; I was the landlord, after
all. His friends were no longer next door, but the place had a
patio! He didn't even use it. He had no reason to rock outdoors of
an evening anymore; after a few years he didn't even rock much.

He permitted himself a single indulgence—a lifelong dream.
His last car was his first Cadillac. It was a dealer demo and a good
deal, but he negotiated the dealers to their knees, until they
agreed to throw in the hubcaps—I think they considered throwing them at his head. He was unfailingly polite and unassuming,
but his tenacity was the last thing to go.

The more I trucked in, the less he threw out. This was our pas
de deux. My own father's daughter, I was too stubborn to see
how futile it was to shower him with goods. Hanging in the bathroom were the towels that had seen me through college—and
they weren't new then!

He was my mother's sole caregiver for years, and whenever I hired someone to help out, he could always find some pretext (politely) to let her go. But finally, with his own health failing, he surrendered. He suffered chronic edema that caused bloating; his liver disease was catching up with him. Now when the call from Clearwater came, it was as likely to be Daddy in the hospital. First he suffered the indignity of live-in help, then round-the-clock help. I paid for that, too.

It was a further wedge between us.

Having someone to care for, someone who needed him, had kept him alive beyond his three score and ten, but it had also worn him down. When he finally became too old and too tired, it took a team of women—three full-time and one part-time—to do what he had done alone.

If you're lucky, you live your life with gratitude for your blessings and for burdens that weren't too heavy. My parents had so much to teach me about grace and gratitude. After one of the many strokes that left my mother shrunken and bent in her hospital bed, the doctor took me aside—I had power of attorney—and Daddy, too, to ask, as the law required, "Do you want heroic measures?"

I didn't need a second to think on it: "No."

"Yes," Daddy said. "You young people look at Mary lying in that bed, and you think, *I wouldn't want to live like that.* But she's not ready to die, and I'm not ready to let her go. We can still have a laugh. We can still find joy."

I pictured them in a room together with two molecules of joy in it. That was enough.

We had never had to grieve for a parent before, Ann and I. Despite all they had suffered and lost, we could always take comfort in having not lost them. But in 1993, when we got the call that

Daddy was back in the hospital we each packed a dark suit. We basically moved into the Morton Plant Hospital in Clearwater.

We knew he knew we were there, but there was little overt communication. He lay so still and quiet, as if he was conserving molecules of energy. But let the doctors come in making rounds and he would greet them, just like the Daddy I'd always known. His heart, lung, and liver functions were all trending down—the only uncertainty was which would fail first. Then one afternoon a doctor looked at his chart and looked at us and said death was imminent—perhaps in minutes.

In a crisis like this, I'm the transportation committee. Plane reservations, train schedules—that's where my mind goes first: Get there! I flew out the door, to the parking lot, to the car, and to the condo where Mom was—only minutes away. I had to get her to the hospital fast, but without scaring her. I said that Daddy could be going soon, and asked if she wanted to say good-bye. From some undamaged part of her brain, she responded as from long experience. She had heard bad news before; she was prepared.

Racing time, it was into the wheelchair, out of the wheelchair, into the car, out of the car, back in the chair—park the car! I didn't know if we'd make it or what we would find when the elevator doors opened on his now-familiar floor. Down the hall and into the room—he was as still as when I had left, but alive. Ann quietly said, "Daddy, Mommy's here." And with that he sat straight up with both arms outstretched!

He lived three more days.

When the end finally came, I was reading by his bed; Ann had stepped out to make a phone call. Daddy made an odd gasp and just as a nurse said to me, "This is it," Ann walked back in the room—she'd forgotten something. She went to the other side of the bed, and we held him in our arms. We assured him we would take care of Mommy; he could go now. And he was gone.

I felt so grateful that this only child had not been alone at the end. Ann said a moving prayer as we lingered by his bed: "Dear

Lord, be with our father, watch over our mother. And thank you for his life, which was a blessing to so many people."

My mother outlived Daddy by three years. Having survived cancer, two heart attacks, and innumerable strokes, she lived to be eighty-two. The week she died, her caregiver left her for a moment to get the mail and, returning, noticed that Mom was not where she'd left her. Mom had scooted her wheelchair a few yards to get a better view of the bay. "I feel like I'm living in a castle," she said.

At night, a car is a capsule hurtling through space. The headlights strain to find the road ahead: probing the edge of the known world. The little red lights are a comforting sign of civilization—they say, *We are not alone.* So do the bright white lights from behind, but ominously.

The antenna catches voices from other states. They are very far away—or we are. The signal drops into the zone of interference. The radio goes off. The passengers drop away. The captain is alone and he's making good time.

Diana, 1997

I had been pursuing Princess Diana for years; everybody had been. She had only been interviewed for British TV with Charles and in formal, stilted affairs. We had more in common than I would have mentioned: I had had a crush on Prince Charles in college. As a Spencer, Diana's lineage was actually more aristocratic than his, yet she couldn't help but appear more human, and the contrast was painful. After the separation, Buckingham Palace was not likely to approve an interview for American TV, but if it did, the rewards would be huge. It was understood that the princess was quietly pursuing an interview opportunity— was even practicing for it secretly, as we now know.

So the pace of the pursuit quickened, and though Barbara Walters had been cultivating a high-profile friendship with Diana, it made sense for me to stay in the race. My interest wasn't only professional but also personal. I felt I knew a little of what her life had been like and that it was not inconceivable that her "people" could make a case for the kind of interview I did: personal but not high-impact. It was still a long shot, but it was worth a pricey ticket on the Concorde just to meet her press secretary for lunch in London. She chose a restaurant so elegant that the presence of a pair of young women at another table drew her attention. She acknowledged them, commenting that *The Sun* or *The Mirror*, one tabloid or the other, must be doing well indeed if reporters could dine out in such style!

After lunch, a car was waiting in the rain for me at the door, along with several men with cameras, who started snapping from the moment I appeared until the car disappeared. I'd been "door-stepped"!—a term of recent coinage to describe the paparazzi waiting in ambush.

My sister was returning from a business trip in the Far East, with a stopover in London the same day, so we arranged to stay at the same hotel and make a weekend of it. I told her about my adventure. She added a dash of intrigue, saying that the previous night her clients had mentioned that photographers were milling about the hotel. I started to put it together. After I'd deplaned, the young man at immigration had inquired, as they do, the nature of my business, the length of my stay, and so on. He recognized NBC and asked whether I was there for an interview. Perhaps a little coyly, I replied, "I hope so." He could see the name and address of my hotel on his form. I presume that photographers at the hotel thought I'd lead them to Diana, and the ones outside in the rain were anticipating the arrival of the princess. Alas, it was just me.

Being doorstepped is creepy. For Diana, it was a way of life. I felt sorry for her.

The chic entrance to Christie's on Park Avenue was blocked by blue police barricades. The most famous woman in the world was coming, and arriving all by myself, I got a little preview of the welcome she would get.

Everybody had to walk a gauntlet of photographers on risers five or six deep on either side of a red carpet stretched from the curb to the door—there was no other way to get in. When I stepped out of my car, it was like the parting of the Red Sea: a thousand strobe lights exploded on either side of me against a chorus of disembodied voices bellowing, "Jane! Jane! Over here! Jane! Jane!" I could barely see where I was going, and I certainly couldn't see the point of all the fuss. Maybe they were just warming up their motor-drives for the main attraction. None of the pictures ever appeared anywhere—a show of Jane Pauley's dresses would not attract much attention, though once, years ago, I found Tommy giving playmates a tour of Mommy's closet.

That's ostensibly why we were there—it was an exhibition of Princess Diana's dresses, which were to be sold at auction to raise money for charity. The event had been the brainstorm of her son William. Stone Phillips was also there, and our agenda was to secure an interview, though by then Barbara Walters seemed to have it locked up.

I'd never seen the likes of it. The opening of the exhibition was one of those "hottest tickets in town" that actually *was*. From every realm—politics, finance, fashion, showbiz, newsbiz—the people came to see the princess in person, and what she would be wearing.

I was hiding. I fled into a phone booth, a very haute phone booth. It was paneled with dark mahogany and had beveled glass windows against which someone with a very broad back had parked himself. I couldn't see anything, but fortunately no one could see me, either. I decided that just in case, I should appear to be calling the desk. So I called Ann Kolbell, my closest associate at NBC for twenty-five years, to give her a commentary. Before long, a flood of lights swept by and the big man in a tuxedo moved on, so I ventured into the mob.

She was much taller than I expected. She was much more than I expected. Her figure was leaner but a lot stronger than I expected, despite a palpable emotional vulnerability that was probably the secret of her human touch.

The orchestration was awesome. She would move or be moved from person to person, never lingering longer than thirty seconds. She would make a comment or listen, appearing genuinely interested. There were a number of people ("Henry! Anna!") I'd see again weeks later in the waiting room of the British Airways Concorde en route to the funeral. I had my turn, and while I didn't get the feeling she'd ever remember what I'd said, or me, or that I'd be hearing from her again, she radiated warmth! I can't remember what I said, either.

Meeting her, I had to blush at my letters on file in Buckingham Palace, how I tried to convey what we'd had in common. Yes, we had children and a hairstyle and a pulse, but that was that. She was very much the aristocrat, but I actually liked her more than I expected to. Then she was swept away, and the crowd thinned out enough to get a look at the dresses. It was hard to imagine a princess sending her garments to be cleaned, but some had the puckered seams to show that they were part of a working wardrobe. As I left, two people told me, separately, that a member of her entourage had been looking for me. I wasn't hiding in the phone booth anymore; I'll just never know what that was about.

Three weeks later she was gone, and the people in the Concorde waiting lounge heading to her funeral no doubt had some reason to feel so much in common with her, too, as the millions who mourned her worldwide felt some fundamental kinship with this famous girl who led a privileged but isolated and sad life. She was cursed with both a mismatched marriage and a mismatched job. She was barely beyond her childhood, an unhappy one, when she married into the most famous family business in the world. As we heard her say in her own words on secret audiotapes, with no training she was fed to the media, without protection, emotional support, or appreciation. Princess or commoner, that was an emotionally life-threatening combination. I don't think it was a coincidence that the dress auction was to benefit her favorite cause—land-mine removal.

Diana had a rare quality that inspired people from all walks of life to connect with her, identify with her, even though she was a princess. I identified with having a public life while being shy, with being young and vulnerable in a high-profile job; and with having children. But she had undergone a transformation. Once Diana's marriage was thoroughly over, she came into her own. She became a woman who knew her strengths.

I was still in the dark, hiding in the phone booth. Getting out more, schmoozing celebrities, working the phones, getting the get—while these things were fundamental expectations for someone in my line of work, they were antithetic to me. The cumulative cost of years of guilt and denial would be paid for with my health. But getting sick would be freeing, too, a turning point. I was beginning to learn my own strengths.

March 2000

I was on vacation again with my family in Florida; still plagued by hives after a year. This time, they arrived in a terrifying swarm.

I had packed as vacation reading Moss Hart's memoir *Act One*. This was a book that had lain at my father's bedside for a number of years—so long that Mom must have dusted it a hundred times. I was curious to know what it was about this book. The day I started *Act One* was the day my hives took an aggressive turn. My throat was swelling up. Until then, I had never thought about being killed by hives. After that, I was encouraged to carry an "epi-pen" at all times.

Back home again and now reading *Act One* for the sheer pleasure of it, I flipped to the back of the book to see how many more pages I still had to savor. I found a list I had scribbled of everything I ate, drank, or touched that day in Florida. Then, returning to Moss Hart's story, at the top of the next page, the very next line said: "I broke out in hives."

I believe it was the single mention of hives in all four-hundred–plus pages. Coincidence? Why, sure. But still . . .

2002

Hives were no longer top priority, and after two years, they finally retreated and disappeared. But nobody knew what the trouble was, hence the medical description "idiopathic." But I was still thinking about them; I knew hives had been the root of my trouble, but what was at the root of the hives? No allergies were ever discovered. Intuitively, I was sure it was not only one thing but a confluence of factors. But I was surprised to find something so starkly obvious. It occurred to me to find out what I had been working on at *Dateline* at the time the hives first reappeared. Scrolling back to my March 1999 computer files, I found a dozen files with the same name: "Daddy."

It was the "Roots" assignment.

My childrearing policy was to keep work and family as separate as church and state, but celebrity cannot be so easily contained— and I wasn't even a "star." ("Mom! Jai said he saw you on the bus!") My picture was rolling around town on the sides of city buses for a while. I don't know that it was a bad thing, but it would be hard to argue it was good—and it had an impact on my children regardless of my vigilance.

My father's alcoholism was also a fact of my childhood, though he took pains to hide it as long as he could. He was the model family man—even-tempered, responsible, and reliable. He was far more likely than most neighborhood dads to be seen at school functions. He was invariably taken for the minister invited to make the invocation. He was never sick. He never missed church. He took care of the house, paid bills on time, avoided debt, saved for the future.

He was married almost fifty years to the same woman, put two children through college, made scores of friends and no enemies. He preserved the placid conventionality of our home life. My sister and I lived in denial about the impact alcoholism had on us as long as we could.

I often think of Daddy in Central Park, for no particular reason. One day walking alone there, I had a little epiphany: He wasn't a tragic figure; resilience was the story of his life! When tragedy struck, and it did, often, he got right up again! But maybe he got up too soon.

PART VIII

Into
the Blue

One summer Sunday morning as I contentedly watched, in my bathrobe, with a cup of coffee in my hand, Garry and the twins were hard at work making a stone path. They dug the soil, collected rocks, poured cement, and set the stones. Tommy, then four, stood watching alongside me. I asked him: "Don't you want to help?" He said: *"I'm never going to do work I have to do; I'm only going to do work I want to do."*

I've been writing from the vantage point of—and mostly for—women my age, give or take. Physical vitality and two generations of feminism have enabled us to be ready to begin again at middle age. The active notion that there is more to come at, or after, midlife is original to our generation.

I haven't written much about my job: The boys in the back room have given me more material about my private life than about my professional life. Having spent thirty years protecting my privacy, to suddenly write such a personal story might take some explaining. It's entirely in the motivation. I always held out for *Dateline* stories that felt like they had some redeeming quality. My instinct told me I had an opportunity to help, and I didn't spend a lot of time second-guessing. Nor do I go anywhere here that I haven't taken someone else in an interview for *Dateline*.

Skywriting—being actively available to moments of recognition, to the portals to insight—has enabled me to discover what was hiding in plain sight. What I'd thought of as purpose*less* wandering turned out to be purpose*ful*, once I started paying attention. My body—my illness—forced me to listen.

· · ·

For many years, inspired by my sister's work as a business executive, I've prowled the business shelves at bookstores looking at books on management, organizations, and job satisfaction. Buckingham and Clifton's *Now, Discover Your Strengths* wasn't the first such book I read—it was more like the twentieth. I don't mean to offer it or any other title as the key to understanding. Because if I've learned anything, it's how customized a journey of self-discovery has to be.

The mystery of the human race begins with the mystery of the human mind. And those backroom boys of mine still know things they haven't revealed to me. But books have helped me recognize how I am organized. For instance, a recent discovery in a book called *Finding Flow*, by Mihaly Csikszentmihalyi, was that "many people don't know which elements of their lives cause stress and which they actually enjoy."

I was thinking about that in relation to my daughter, Rickie, not getting enough of her mommy. The *Today* hours had been perfect when I had babies. I left before dawn and could be back before noon oftentimes. (The nanny we hired was a little alarmed to see me walk in the door at midmorning on her first day!) But the older the kids got, the more the job was in direct competition. I could see the day coming when my homework would arrive at the same time they got home from school. The idea that my children were being held hostage to my contract was very real to me. I fought so hard to be able to leave *Today* and go home. But when I lost, I started feeling better. Why?

Because there can be a fine line between something that causes stress and something we enjoy, and when I left *Today* I crossed that line. One of my happiest times was the period between *Today* and *Dateline*, during the ill-fated little show called *Real Life*. For one thing, the title itself almost defined my interests. As a reporter, what has always interested me most is the thing we used to pejoratively label "soft news"—anything to do with women, health, well-being, education, and the everyday choices and challenges people make and face, and why some are successful and life-enhancing and others are not. Exploring my family history was being a reporter in the sense that I'm the best at. Two additional factors were different: There were no more fabulous but faraway junkets to compete with my obligations at home. And my hours were normal—no more bifurcated workday: showtime in the morning, homework at night.

I noticed all the arrows had turned and were pointing in a new direction. My parents were gone; I was on the other side of a biological change. It had been a more turbulent passage than I was expecting. Life comes, ready or not. And kids leave the same way.

2002

I put two kids in college in one week. I didn't cry or make a scene or one of Mom's famous speeches. I just lingered. First, I folded all of Ross's T-shirts and lined them up by color; then I went after the chaos of cords and cables from his computer, microwave, CD player, refrigerator, clock radio, lamp, and TV. I got them untangled and began winding them neatly with little twist ties. I was actually underneath the desk when I became aware of an awkward silence that said *Anyone here who isn't somebody's roommate should go now.*

I had a second chance—Rickie shared a suite with five girls and, for a while, it appeared, six parents. The fathers were mostly occupied with hardware—hooking up computers and assembling bookcases—while we mothers mostly tended to software—socks, sheets, and towels. I resolved not to be the last one to leave. Reports were true. I had heard that a daughter who wouldn't be seen in public with her mother in high school will unabashedly hold her hand in college—if only while leading her out of the room and back to the car.

For me, it wasn't only about letting go. It was about going back. Everything about college looked appealing. I wanted to change my major. Middle-aged women have a lot in common with kids—all of us on the cusp of the unknown: enticing and scary.

Sometimes I dream about my parents and awaken with sweet memories of a visit.

They are always living in a house I don't remember. In one dream we were even shopping for real estate together, Mom walking from place to place. In another dream she had a part-time job. She had been an invalid the last sixteen years of her life, so to see her doing so well made me feel grateful and optimistic. My father was generally as I remember him. I hug him in my dreams, and his shoulders under my arms feel exactly right—the extra weight he put on, the precise height of my arms up around his neck, the sweater he wore almost every day, though he lived in Florida.

These dreams leave me feeling warm and happy. But one day the dog woke me up before my dream was done, and all I felt was that I was missing my parents. The streets were shiny and wet when the dog and I went out—only a few people in rain gear were about.

Literally wiping a tear from my eye, I returned home to notice that Garry had left an envelope addressed to me on the kitchen table. In it was a letter that said:

Attached is a copy of your estrogen profile. You are well within menopausal range. . . .

How often does menopause arrive by mail? I sat down and had a little cry.

During parents' weekend, colleges provide activities to make them feel welcome and keep them out of their kids' hair. Garry and I chose a lecture called "Entrepreneurship and Good Work," wondering what "good work" meant. I listened closely as the professor explained that the first characteristic of good work is "alignment"—that is, feeling aligned with the mission of the enterprise. The second is "consistency": You should be reinforced in that alignment consistently.

After that, I stopped listening. I knew I was out of alignment. Several weeks later, I told Neal Shapiro, now president of NBC News, that I was ready to move on. Of course, he wondered where to—and I had no answer. I only knew it was time to go.

After my decision to leave *Dateline* was announced, I got a call from Barbara Walters. I was suddenly a get. And for the second time in my life, I would be famous for knowing it was time to stop. But this time there was no hint of rancor, no victim or villain. It would not have made a good *Dateline* story, I told my colleagues, because there was no conflict. NBC and I were parting as old friends, with mutual respect.

My reasons for leaving *Dateline* were honest, and the subsequent accolades, though excessive, were not extravagant. I enjoyed far more praise for my conduct than for my work, which was about right; I am not one of the great journalists of my time. The person I heard being celebrated accurately described the person I at least aspired to be. I allowed myself to enjoy it, which for me was something of a first! I didn't mind a bit that my kids might see the article that said their mother was "universally liked and admired."

"I'm comfortable with change," I kept telling people. "I make bold decisions. I have faith in the unknown." My longtime associate and friend Ann Kolbell found the going harder, especially when change was uninvited. "Aren't you at all nostalgic?" she asked me, sighing plaintively after days immersed in weathered clippings, decades-old mail, and pictures from travel all over the world—some of it done together. I reminded her of the oldest joke in my book: "I'm not archival; I don't even sweep in that room." It was funny only to the extent that it was true. It was a moment when we both understood how profoundly different we are—and not just because I felt energized by the unknown.

I revisited the book *Now, Discover Your Strengths* with her. We both took the test; this time I wasn't sick. Ann's strengths were all about relationships and connecting and finding harmony. Her results seemed on the money to me; not surprisingly, she came off as a wonderful human being.

I sounded like G.I. Jane. According to the list, these were my strengths:

Strategic: analyzing information and seeing the big picture.

Activator: someone who's quick to pull the trigger on decisions—one–two–three: fire!

Ideation: generating ideas.

Command: a sense of presence that compels others (not necessarily leadership ability). I have zero leadership ability.

Communicator: Well, that one's obvious.

Though few people would relate to his meaning, Mark Twain said: "Work and play are words used to describe the same thing under different conditions."

I'm trying to imagine my grandmother defining her work as play, but I think she came closer to having it all than I have. She came to it without resistance. She enjoyed the emotional rewards of doing well what she did best, and she was richly paid in appreciation. Is there any doubt she was in alignment with her work as a farmwife and mother? She had set the goals—to raise three daughters who wouldn't have to work that hard!

Ironically, the lesson my mother learned from her mother's example is that a good wife and mother shows her love by getting a lot of work done. My mother may have come to it without resistance, but she got fewer rewards than she might have from work more consistent with her own strengths, interests, and abilities. As a result, her work was not fulfilling; it was emotionally draining. Meanwhile, I learned from my mother's example that a good mother is always supposed to be there. We both fell short of our own expectations and suffered for it; so did our families.

As my own daughter recognized, a good mother has to be there emotionally as well as physically, and when an unhappy mother is not fully present, a little girl can feel like she doesn't get enough of her mommy. And that goes for daddies too.

New York, 2004

I used to say that my life, meaning my career and its attendant perquisites, was wasted on me—I thought it was a joke. There was more than a kernel of truth to the statement. I certainly don't regret being a bad celebrity, but I did squander many opportunities to be my most creative, productive, and happy. And NBC got shortchanged, too, because people who enjoy their work do it better and more productively; being happy is the bonus. Among the hardest things I've had to admit—privately or publicly—were my tangled feelings about my work. But I don't think I'm alone. When NBC announced I was leaving the network after twenty-seven years, I was stunned by the attention this news got. Somebody called me the "poster child for second acts." I inspired a number of people to do the same.

After I'd finally done it, was free and clear and leaving NBC on the best of terms, not a month later I turned around and headed right back into the old familiar barn. Or as Garry joked, at my expense, "After twenty-seven years at NBC, my wife made the courageous decision to leave *Dateline* and join an entirely different department at NBC." In a famous televised interview, Prince Charles once explained to his countrymen that his marriage to Diana had failed, "us both having tried." That particular phrase stuck with me. I think the fact that my marriage to NBC thrives in its fourth decade proves that both parties kept trying.

For years, my sister and I have enjoyed relaxing together at spa retreats. And the conversations I've found endlessly interesting were about her work; her expertise is in management. I was fascinated both by her experiences and by the books she packed in her suitcase. But I see now that my own choices in extracurricular reading had a deeper motivation: I wanted work happiness for myself.

At some point, not long ago, I realized the wisdom of Tommy's statement (at the age of four) about "work I want to do . . ." And I also realized that the work you *want* to do might not be that different from the stuff you *have* to do.

The Jane Pauley Show, obviously, is something new for me, but not a total reinvention. I've never done a daytime show before, but I've been Jane Pauley my whole life—though I've made it harder than necessary. Without a doubt, but for Skywriting, making that decision would have been inconceivable; nevertheless, it was a hard decision to make. I'll tell you when I made it.

It was the last interview I did for *Dateline*, with one of my heroes, Michael J. Fox. We have some history together—from *Today* to *Real Life* to *Dateline*: I interviewed him before he was a star and again after he became a superstar, a father, an author, a Parkinson's sufferer. I was thrilled that he agreed to be the centerpiece of my final appearance on *Dateline* in May 2003. I had just enumerated his recent accomplishments—a book, a movie, a fourth baby, millions raised for the Michael J. Fox Foundation for Parkinson's research. Then I said, "Knowing how stress exacerbates your symptoms, if it was me, I'd be relaxin', takin' it easy, conserving my energy."

He said, "What would you be conserving your energy *for*?"

The question pinged around in my head. I thought, *What are you conserving your energy for?*

There was not a unanimous vote of confidence from the backroom boys. But I was pleased that the minority inside me was voted down; it has held too much power for too long. The choice was between conserving my energy while squandering an opportunity or taking a bold leap of faith and adapting to the consequences as they appeared—and I was going to leap. Ironically, leaping into the unknown and going home again were the same things!

There has never been such a preoccupation with celebrity as in our culture right now. I've always been suspicious of celebrity seekers. A psychoanalyst whose own father was world famous concluded: "It might be accurate to say that the public image reflects what the private person most longs to be." The paradox of fame, if I understand correctly, is that people seek recognition to compensate for some psychological inadequacy—the reverse of their public image. When I first read about this five years ago, I felt confident that it didn't apply to me, because I became famous by luck and timing and was still wondering, all those years later, how I got here. And anyway, who would want to be famous for being ordinary? If I have worked to create an image, that was it.

I have a paper trail of testimonials going back decades that follows the same line: "doesn't put on airs"; "hasn't changed"; "kept her head"; "still our lil' ol' Janie." I had never seen audience research about me until recently. It said the words most associated with my name were *authenticity* and *genuineness.* I was pleased. Perhaps it was a clever (but unconscious) strategy to win recognition without looking like I wanted it. From WMAQ in Chicago through *Today* and *Dateline,* I patrolled the boundary between credibility and celebrity, avoiding red carpets and not collecting famous friends. I declined invitations to make cameo appearances in movies. I sent regrets when CBS sent an invitation for me to appear as myself on the *Murphy Brown* baby shower episode, not that I was sorely missed.

In the early 1990s, I put my chunky jewelry away, including my favorite earrings, which, I realize now, looked like propellers attached to my head. This was a private statement against artifice. I also stopped coloring my hair for a year. I got over that. The impulse to be myself—not more, not less—was expressed in story assignments. I was not afraid to "just say no," even at the risk of overhearing, as I did: "Jane will say no. She always says no."

I've been practicing medicine without a license, diagnosing my friends and colleagues and guests, for so long that I'm comfortable speculating about myself: I was so preoccupied with "just be yourself" because I wasn't sure who that was. There are worse ways to express insecurity. And I don't think I'm alone in feeling that way this late in life.

My career has taken me so many places, but now I feel like I'm going places on my own initiative. Now that *Skywriting* is about done, I'm looking forward to having fewer insights. Whether I live happily ever after remains to be seen. I lay awake last night worrying again. It helps me to know so many other people do that, too. On the show, we'll be doing segments about insomnia. That we're in this together will be one of the show's themes.

My old friends my weaknesses are still milling about, of course, but they have lost their powers of enchantment. I see them in proper proportion, and they no longer obscure my strengths, which have toiled in darkness, unbidden and unnamed. Until now, Activator and Command have operated reflexively and defensively. I picture them in suits of armor and bearing battle-axes. They were pretty blunt instruments. I think that was why Garry blurted out, about Activator: "Are you sure that's a strength?"

Having discovered and recognized them, my challenge will be learning how to use my strengths productively. They have to be civilized and trained to move about in public confidently, not furtively. Maybe I should try to imagine Command and Activator in decorative uniforms, à la Gilbert and Sullivan, so I remember that they're readily at hand but deploy them with humor and humility. Command needs to show some restraint, and Activator doesn't have to be quite so quick on the trigger.

I look forward to giving Communicator some freedom. When I was younger it was sometimes said that I was "too careful." The looser persona that allegedly arrived at the same time the twins did was in refreshing contrast. What caused this transformation? I had a life, I had a home, and it was teeming with people! I didn't have to be careful because I had less to lose, and the reward for being less careful was success. I think it was Communicator taunting Activator to pull the trigger and say yes to *The Jane Pauley Show*. I've told my kids that no matter what happens—success or something less—I'm proud I had the courage to say yes.

Strategic is the grown-up in this crowd of strengths-in-training; I've counted on her in the past and had confidence in her judgment.

Ideation is my idea of work defined as play, to paraphrase Mark Twain. I didn't know her as a strength, per se, but as an old friend. I love sowing the seeds of ideas and seeing them sprout and grow and branch out to be harvested by the armload. I already see that brainstorming show ideas will be one of my favorite parts of the workday now. Heretofore, this piece was missing in my work life, because heretofore no program had ever been called *The Jane Pauley Show*. I'm hoping that my being organically involved in defining our mission will guarantee that I'm in alignment and that it will provide the consistent reinforcement of that alignment—the first and second criteria of "good work."

It's as close to work I *want* to do as I need it to be.

Epilogue

From a high window, I'm looking west toward the Hudson River and miles and miles beyond—not a cloud in the blue morning sky. I feel more clarity now than when I began *Skywriting*, but I'm under no illusions. Who knows what's next to come out of the blue? The world has not become spontaneously organized to make accommodations for my weaknesses while nurturing my newly discovered strengths.

No one can tell me whether I'll ever have another bipolar episode, but no one can guarantee I won't, and nothing would tempt me to take a chance and stop taking lithium—which is just a salt. Some do think it's worth the risk, and I can almost understand why. I remember once feeling like Sophia Loren! The feeling was fleeting but vivid. We were dining at a great Italian restaurant—but not that great! I think my brain was reaching for the phrase *la dolce vita!* and overreached. But I'm okay with never feeling like Sophia Loren again, and I can live without euphoria. I never liked roller coasters or movie thrillers, anyway. The image of Jane Pauley at the end of a bungee cord is almost funny. But not quite.

My moods ebb and flow like anyone's, though I keep a closer watch on mine than most people. I'm alert to signs that I feel too tired or too angry, but especially too good. Most people could safely experience the sequence of medicine from steroids to anti-depressants that got me into such trouble; my reaction was not common, but I'm far from alone. I see a lot about it in the press now. However, I'm not on a crusade. It's good to keep things in proportion: Awareness is healthy; alarm is not.

I doubt I will ever be able to say, "I come to it with *no* resistance," but I am definitely facing my life with *less* resistance. Self-knowledge won't eliminate the burdens of life, but it can lighten the unnecessary baggage we drag around. That's quite a lot.

There are no charmed lives, only lives.

Appendix

Bipolar Disorder

Bipolar disorder (manic–depression) is an illness recognized in antiquity, well described by Hellenistic physicians and codified by the German, French, and British alienists of the Enlightenment. Today it is successfully treated when appropriate pharmacotherapy is made available.

The illness can be triggered by a variety of physiological and psychological stressors. When the illness appears to "come out of the blue," we assume that significant biological factors are at work. When the manias and depressions are classic in nature, we describe the illness as bipolar type I. In some cases, the depressions are classic, but the manias are mild and nonpsychotic (known as hypomania), and we describe this presentation as bipolar type II. On the other hand, there are instances in which medications, such as antidepressants and steroids, have been prescribed for the treatment of depression or other medical disorders. These medications can cause depression, if not already present, as well as induce mania or hypomania; we describe these cases, such as the case described in *Skywriting*, as bipolar type III.

Lithium carbonate, carbamazepine, and valproic acid are the mainstays of current pharmacotherapy, but atypical antipsychotics and other anti–epileptic mood–stabilizing medications also appear to be useful. The successful treatment of bipolar disorder depends upon its recognition through differential diagnosis, followed by comprehensive care, which can include hospitalization, psychotherapy, psycho–education, and family involvement, along with drug therapy.

A growing number of support groups and educational resources are available. The National Alliance for the Mentally Ill (NAMI 1–800–950–6264) is an excellent starting point for treatment referrals, general information, and advocacy. Physician-referral services, affiliated with major medical centers, can direct patients to knowledgeable practitioners. The Internet offers dozens of sites providing services, information, and points of view. Some caution and skepticism are appropriate when seeking information on the Internet, since reason, truth, and science can be in short supply on some sites. Mayoclinic.com is a good site to find useful information, as is the National Institute of Mental Health's website, www.nimh.nih.gov.

Prognosis is good in 85 percent of patients, and even when treatments fail, there is an absolute trend for individual episodes of mania and depression to resolve over time. When confronted with this illness, be patient with yourself or with your afflicted family member, and whenever possible, be proactive and courageous.

Frank Miller, M.D.

Acknowledgments

Ann Pauley, Kate Medina, Wayne Kabak, Maureen Fitzgerald, Gina Centrello, Libby McGuire, Veronica Windholz, Danielle Posen, Frankie Jones, James Danly, Holly Webber, Jessica Kirshner, Carole Lowenstein, Janet Wygal, Gene Mydlowski, Carol Schneider, Benjamin Dreyer, Richard Elman, Lisa Feuer, Ann Kolbell, Martha Davidson, John Meek, Diane Keaton, Joyce Small, Melinda Miller, Patsy Stephenson, Janet Ingram, David Stanford, Nancy Kriplen, Marilyn Preston, Jann Wenner, Frank Rich, Tom Magill, Dr. Steven Potkin, Dr. Arnold Cooper, Jeanne Fenn, and Michelle Trudeau.

ABOUT THE AUTHOR

JANE PAULEY began her broadcasting career in 1972 at her hometown Indianapolis station, WISH-TV. She joined NBC in 1975 as the first woman ever to co-anchor a weeknight evening newscast at NBC's WMAQ-TV in Chicago. She began her thirteen-year tenure on NBC's *Today* in 1976. In 1992, NBC News launched the newsmagazine show *Dateline NBC*, with Pauley as co-anchor. After eleven years, her final appearance aired as the acclaimed special "Jane Pauley: Signing Off." She is the host of *The Jane Pauley Show*.

Pauley has won many awards, including the Radio-Telvision News Directors Association's Paul White Award for her lifetime contribution to electronic journalism and their Leonard Zeidenberg First Amendment Award, and the National Press Foundation's Sol Taishoff Award of Excellence in Broadcast Journalism. She lives in New York City.

ABOUT THE TYPE

The text of this book was set in Nofret, a typeface designed in 1986 by Gudrun Zapf–von Hesse especially for the Berthold foundry.

ABOUT THE TYPE

The text of this book was set in Nofret, a typeface designed in 1986 by Gudrun Zapf–von Hesse especially for the Berthold foundry.